FIFTH WORLD CONFERENCE ON INFORMATION SECURITY EDUCATION

T0235514

IFIP – The International Federation for Information Processing

IFIP was founded in 1960 under the auspices of UNESCO, following the First World Computer Congress held in Paris the previous year. An umbrella organization for societies working in information processing, IFIP's aim is two-fold: to support information processing within its member countries and to encourage technology transfer to developing nations. As its mission statement clearly states,

> *IFIP's mission is to be the leading, truly international, apolitical organization which encourages and assists in the development, exploitation and application of information technology for the benefit of all people.*

IFIP is a non-profitmaking organization, run almost solely by 2500 volunteers. It operates through a number of technical committees, which organize events and publications. IFIP's events range from an international congress to local seminars, but the most important are:

• The IFIP World Computer Congress, held every second year;
• Open conferences;
• Working conferences.

The flagship event is the IFIP World Computer Congress, at which both invited and contributed papers are presented. Contributed papers are rigorously refereed and the rejection rate is high.

As with the Congress, participation in the open conferences is open to all and papers may be invited or submitted. Again, submitted papers are stringently refereed.

The working conferences are structured differently. They are usually run by a working group and attendance is small and by invitation only. Their purpose is to create an atmosphere conducive to innovation and development. Refereeing is less rigorous and papers are subjected to extensive group discussion.

Publications arising from IFIP events vary. The papers presented at the IFIP World Computer Congress and at open conferences are published as conference proceedings, while the results of the working conferences are often published as collections of selected and edited papers.

Any national society whose primary activity is in information may apply to become a full member of IFIP, although full membership is restricted to one society per country. Full members are entitled to vote at the annual General Assembly, National societies preferring a less committed involvement may apply for associate or corresponding membership. Associate members enjoy the same benefits as full members, but without voting rights. Corresponding members are not represented in IFIP bodies. Affiliated membership is open to non-national societies, and individual and honorary membership schemes are also offered.

FIFTH WORLD CONFERENCE ON INFORMATION SECURITY EDUCATION

Proceedings of the IFIP TC11 WG 11.8, WISE 5, 19 to 21 June 2007, United States Military Academy, West Point, New York, USA

Edited by

Lynn Futcher
Centre of Information Security Studies, Nelson Mandela Metropolitan University
Port Elizabeth, South Africa

Ronald Dodge
United States Military Academy
West Point, New York, USA

 Springer

Fifth World Conference on Information Security Education

Edited by L. Futcher and R. Dodge

p. cm. (IFIP International Federation for Information Processing, a Springer Series in Computer Science)

ISSN: 1571-5736 / 1861-2288 (Internet)

ISBN 978-1-4419-4458-0   eISBN: 13: 978-0-387-73268-5
Printed on acid-free paper

9 8 7 6 5 4 3 2 1
springer.com

Conference Chairs:

General Chair	Daniel Ragsdale
	United States Military Academy, West Point, NY USA
Program Chair	Natalia Miloslavskaya
	Moscow Engineering Physics Institute (State University), Moscow, Russia
Finance/Registration Chair	Ronald Dodge
	United States Military Academy, West Point, NY USA
Local Support Chair	Greg Conti
	United States Military Academy, West Point, NY USA
Publication Chair	Lynn Futcher
	Nelson Mandela Metropolitan University, Port Elizabeth, South Africa

Conference Program Committee (in alphabetical order):

Helen Armstrong	Curtin University, Bentley, Western Australia
Colin Armstrong	Gailaad Pty Ltd, Perth, Western Australia
Matt Bishop	University of California, Davis CA, USA
Curt Carver	United States Military Academy, West Point, NY USA
Ronald Dodge	United States Military Academy, West Point, NY USA
Lynette Drevin	North-West University, Potchefstroom, South Africa
Steve Furnell	University of Plymouth, Plymouth, United Kingdom
Lynn Futcher	Nelson Mandela Metropolitan University, South Africa
Edler Johannes	Upper Austria University, Austria
Vasilis Katos	University of Portsmouth, Portsmouth, United Kingdom
Hennie Kruger	North-West University, Potchefstroom, South Africa
Phillip Lock	University of South Australia, Adelaide, South Australia
Javier Lopez	University of Malaga, Malaga, Spain
Vashek Matyas	Masaryk University, Brno,Czech Republic
Natalia Miloslavskaya	Moscow Engineering Physics Institute, Moscow, Russia
Daniel Ragsdale	United States Military Academy, West Point, NY USA
Jill Slay	University of South Australia, Mawson Lakes, Australia
Katsikas Socrates	Aegean University, Mytilene, Greece
Chris Steketee	University of South Australia, Mawson Lakes, Australia
Min Surp Rhee	Dankook Universioty, Seoul, Korea

Organizing Committee:

Carol Spisso	United States Military Academy, West Point, NY USA
George Corrigan	United States Military Academy, West Point, NY USA
Erik Dean	United States Military Academy, West Point, NY USA

Preface

Welcome to the Fifth World Conference on Information Security Education (WISE) held at the United States Military Academy in West Point, New York, USA. The theme of this workshop focuses on three primary discussion topics:

- How to Design Computer Security Experiments,
- The Role of Information Security Industry Training and Accreditation in Tertiary Education, and
- Industry Support to Training and Education.

These thee discussion topics are the focus of three sub-working groups for the conference. The discussion lead for each topic presents the topic and hypothesis in a plenary session to the WISE attendees. The sub-working groups then break out to discuss each topic. The working group phase of the workshop ends with the discussion leads presenting the results of each sub-working group in a plenary session. After the working group sessions, selected authors will present research results that are included in this proceeding.

The WISE conferences provide an international forum for professionals in industry, the academia, defense and government organisations to share their theories, knowledge and experiences in information security education and training. The WISE 5 conference is no exception, and includes submissions from across the globe including the USA, UK, Russia, Greece, South Africa, Sweden and Australia. The WISE conferences are organized by the Working Group 11.8 Information Security Education, under the IFIP Technical Committee 11 (TC11) on Security and Protection in Information Processing Systems. Previous WISE conferences include:

- WISE 1 held in Stockholm, Sweden in 1999;
- WISE 2 held in Perth, Australia in 2001;
- WISE 3 held in Monterey, California, USA in 2003; and
- WISE 4 held in Moscow, Russia in 2005.

All papers included in these proceedings have undergone blind reviews by members of the international committee. A special word of thanks is due to all the members of the international program committee for the time that they dedicated to reviewing these papers and providing valuable feedback to the authors.

We look forward to WISE 6, to be held in 2009. The location is still to be determined and will be published on the working group website (http://www.118.ifip.info) as soon as it is determined. We would like to encourage all those interested in information security education to submit papers and panel proposals to this forthcoming conference.

A sincere word of thanks to all those who contributed towards the success of WISE 5!

Dr. Daniel Ragsdale
IFIP WG 11.8 Chair

Table of Contents

Refereed Papers

Invited Papers

Author Index

Stefan Lindskog (Karlstad University, Sweden) 73
Stefan.Lindskog@kau.se

Phillip Lock (University of South Australia) 113
Phillip.Lock@unisa.edu.au

Leonardo A. Martucci (Karlstad University, Sweden) 73
leonardo.martucci@kau.se

Jeff Mattson (SEI, Carnegie Mellon University, Pittsburgh) 81
jmattson@cmu.edu

Natalia Miloslavskaya (Moscow Engineering Physics Institute, Russia) 87
milmur@mephi.edu

Kjell Näckro (Stockholm University/Royal Institute of Technology, Sweden).25, 95
kjellna@dsv.su.se

Sean Peisertn *(University of California, Davis)* 141
peisert@cs.ucsd.edu

Matthew Simon *(University of South Australia, Australia)* 105
matthew.simon@unisa.edu.au

Jill Slay (University of South Australia, Australia) 105
Jill.Slay@unisa.edu.au

Chris Steketee (University of South Australia) 113
Chris.Steketee@cs.unisa.edu.au

Tjaart Steyn (North-West University, South Africa) 33
Tjaart.Steyn@nwu.ac.za

*Eleftheria Stougiannou (Athens University of Economics and Business, Greec*e).49
estoug@aueb.gr

Caroline Strevens (University of Portsmouth, UK) 65
caroline.strevens@port.ac.uk

Anatoly Temkin (Metropolitan College, Boston University, Boston) 57,121
temkin@bu.edu

*Marianthi Theoharidou (Athens University of Economics and Business, Greec*e)..49
mtheohar@aueb.gr

Alexander I.Tolstoy (Moscow Engineering Physics Institute, Russia) 87
tolstoy@mephi.ru

Rossouw von Solms (Nelson Mandela Metropolitan University, South Africa)... 41
Rossouw.VonSolms@nmmu.ac.za

Clare Wilson (University of Portsmouth, UK) 65
clare.wilson@port.ac.uk

Stephen Wolthusen (Royal Holloway, University of London, UK) 129
stephen.wolthusen@rhul.ac.uk

Louise Ynström (DSV, Kista, Stockholm, Sweden) 9
Louise@dsv.su.se

Tanya Zlateva (Metropolitan College, Boston University, Boston) 57
zlateva@bu.edu

An Analysis of Computer Forensic Practitioners Perspectives on Education and Training Requirements

Colin J. Armstrong

Gailaad Pty Ltd, Perth,
Western Australia
ColinArmstrong@gailaad.com

Abstract. It could be argued that the academic perspective of computer forensic practitioner requirements reflecting the thinking world (and is based on scientific methods) does not accurately reflect those requirements considered important by some people universities would desire as students, the computer forensic practitioners. This paper presents an analysis of data collected from full time practitioners representing three perspectives; military, law enforcement, and forensic scientist. It also examines the needs of practitioners and compares these with academic contributions intended to meet these needs.

Keywords: Academic education programs, Vendor training courses, practitioner education and training needs.

1 Introduction

Much has been written about the importance of evidence integrity but it is the credibility of the forensic practitioner called as an expert witness that may be crucial to the outcome of a case [1]. The most important tool in any computer forensic practitioner's kitbag is their personal integrity. Once doubt is cast upon a practitioner's personal integrity, it matters little how well they conduct their duties. A court or jury may have sufficient doubt of the practitioner's abilities, impartiality, or intentions as to render a successful prosecution impractical. Undertaking and engaging in training and educational programs form an important aspect of developing the perceived integrity of a forensic practitioner.

Both universities and other training and educational providers have long understood the importance of meeting these needs and offer a multitude of courses designed to facilitate meeting student's desired learning outcomes. At Curtin University, Western Australia, programs have an underlying philosophy that should produce a graduate with a set of essential generic skills intended to help them become a "problem solver" first, and a specialist domain expert second [7]. Teaching computer forensics at Curtin University is intended primarily to meet industry demands where the combination of academic research, teaching and training to support industry and law enforcement should improve confidence and credibility of investigators [2].

Slade [14] reiterates the risk that findings and opinions may be dismissed by a court where a computer forensic expert cannot prove sufficient knowledge, education, skill and experience. Kruse and Heiser [11] state that specialists in the field need to

Please use the following format when citing this chapter:

Armstrong, C., 2007, in IFIP International Federation for Information Processing, Volume 237, Fifth World Conference on Information Security Education, eds. Futcher, L., Dodge, R., (Boston: Springer), pp. 1–8.

be flexible and engage in continually learning, and Vatis [15], Littlejohn and Tittel [12], and Warren [16], remind us that by working together, researchers in academia, industry, and government can give our public servants and practitioners the tools skills and knowledge they need to address issues of critical public security. Students however tend to be locked into solution based skills and therefore have difficulty in understanding the 'real' problems of the end-users. Methodologies they learn have solutions and solution notions embedded in them that make it difficult to consider the real nature of problems. Jayaratna [10] defined these as "solution driven opportunities seeking methodologies." Armstrong and Jayaratna [7] also discuss the problem of practitioners finding it difficult to recognize the changes taking place in their own specialist field because they have mastered a set of skills which they are reluctant to sacrifice or to master a new set of skills because of the time investment required.

At the same time those not necessarily concerned with integrity have at their disposal the Internet which holds the capacity to provide the facilities for people with criminal intent to associate and exchange intelligence and acquire skills [4]. Roast, Lavender and Wisniewski [13] state that criminal exploitation of new technologies has brought about three main results: new forms of crime, more traditional forms of crime being committed in new ways that increase benefits or reduce risks to offender, and the more general use of the technologies by offenders, to organise, to communicate, and to shield their activities from surveillance. Eurim [9], reports that the Internet is attractive to criminals because it provides opportunities for stealth and anonymity with the opportunity to automate and organise multiple crimes whilst remaining unseen and possibly undetected.

The problem situation is compounded by the recognition of the perception that exiting solutions are inadequate. Broersma [8] states that the criminal justice system, particularly in the UK, is ill-equipped to handle computer related crime, emphasising that among other challenges, the investigation of crimes require better technical skills. Whilst law enforcement computer forensic practitioners strive to maintain high levels of skill competencies, the majority of police officers are not highly trained in computing and those with a good knowledge of computers or specialist skills in electronic evidence rarely attend the initial investigation at the scene of a crime [5]. This invariably results in vital electronic evidence on computer systems and electronic devices being either overlooked or unwittingly contaminated.

Often computer forensic practitioners have to rely on the police officer in the field to seize and protect the evidence with the attendant risk that a mistake at the scene could cause loss of credibility to the computer forensics investigating officer in any subsequent legal hearing [2].

That academia can provide skills based solutions to law enforcement field offices successfully is discussed by Armstrong and Russo [5]. A significant contributor to the successful outcome of the training project used in preparation to Operation Auxin was that it closely preceded the police operation. Operation Auxin, which resulted in the arrest of approximately 200 people, was the Australian part of the September 2004 US - FBI Operation Falcon, a cooperative international law enforcement operation against organized paedophilia. Detectives and uniformed police faced their in the field 'practical examination' when they were forced to apply the knowledge in situ shortly after undertaking training. There was some concern that had the period between the training and practical application been longer the success of the operation may not have been so high. Feedback from the operation participants reinforced the opinion that the constantly changing nature of equipment and media containing potential electronic evidence makes the need for frequent updated training essential [5].

Eurim [9] together with the UK Institute for Public Policy Research (IPPR) recommend greater training opportunities for police in e-crime and computer forensics stating "New skills are required at all levels within the police and supporting services to enable investigators and forensics experts to trace and analyse criminal activities that involve computers and networks and to gather intelligence from them. New and different techniques are needed to ensure the provenance of evidence in digital form" [9].

2   The Challenge

This then is the problem situation, law enforcement in general and practitioners in particular face both rapidly evolving scientific technology together with a rapidly changing and opportunistic criminal, whilst being required to maintain high levels of competency and enduring a reluctance to abandon mastered skills in order to attain new replacement skills. It is into this mix that both academia and vendors attempt to provide ideal solutions. Because sufficient international data has not been collected and analysed, it is not practical to accurately know all practitioner requirements leading both academia and vendors to provide only the best they can. This paper offers an insight into the practitioner requirements based on data collected from a variety of computer forensic practitioners. None of the practitioners participating in this Survey were students at Curtin University, and of those engaged in university studies were undertaken on a part time basis whilst in full time employment.

3   Practitioner Survey Results and Analysis

Data discussed and presented in this paper is drawn as a subset from a larger survey. Data was collected from practitioner respondents by means of an individually recorded semi-structured interview process [3]. All participants practiced in Australia with the exception of one USA based forensic scientist. Only practitioners employed in a full time capacity were included in the Survey. The three perspectives; military, law enforcement, and forensic scientist, of collected practitioner respondents data is represented in Figure 1.

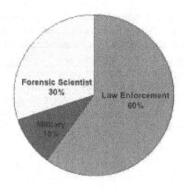

Fig. 1. Respondent Practitioners

The validity of practitioner respondent's entitlement to participate and provide data in the interview process is justified by their responses to the questions shown in Figure 2. Figures 3 and 4 depict years of experience and number of cases worked.

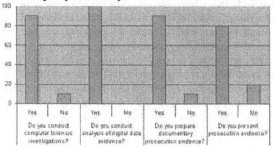

Fig. 2. Clarification of Respondent Practitioner Roles

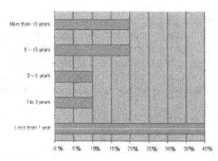

Fig. 3. Respondent Practitioners Experience: Years

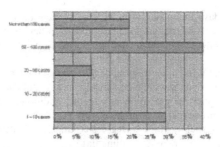

Fig. 4. Respondent Practitioners Experience: Cases

While Figures 1 2 3 and 4 provide an indication of respondent practitioner's proficiency, it is not practicable to estimate an individual's level of competency. All of the practitioners interviewed expressed the opinion that it is desirable that there be a system by which they may determine their personal level of competence [3]. Such a system could permit a practitioner to support a claim of their competency when being assessed by peers, superiors and the Court. While such a system need not be complex it should both provide a uniform or consistent measure whereby they can demonstrate their proficiency and advancement of their skills over a period of time and be internationally recognised, but that discussion is a matter for another paper. This paper focuses on the responses collected from respondent practitioners pertaining to their expressed opinions relating to their previous and desired future training and education which was but one section of the multi-section survey undertaken.

The section of the survey relating to vendor training consisted of a numb er of questions, the first being: "What short training or educational courses have you undertaken that directly relates to computer forensic and digital data evidence analysis ?"

Table 1. Short Training Courses Attended in Order of Popularity.

1	SMART - Advanced
2	FTK Advanced
3	FTK Intro
4	Encase Intro
5	White Wolf Haking 101 / 102
6	Compumatics Cert. Comp Engineer – RS101
7	SMART - Intro & Advanced
8	RedHat RHCT
9	Encase Intermediate
10	Encase Intermediate & Advanced
11	EnCase – Intro & Intermediate
12	SMART - Intro
13	ITAC Applied Hacking
14	Ernst & Young: Extreme Hacking
15	Advanced NTFS
16	Beta release of an in house tool Training Course

100% of respondent practitioners attended multiple short training courses specifically identifying 16 of these. These short training courses ranged in duration from 3 to 20 days with 5 days being the norm with an average duration of 9.6 days. The short training courses undertaken are presented by order of popularity in Table 1 showing the course attended by the most practitioners as being the most popular.

Question 2 asked, "What other training or educational courses have you undertaken that you believe assists you in computer forensic and digital data evidence analysis?" Again, 100% of respondent practitioners attended additional education or training courses identifying three types of programs;

(a.) University (Bachelor, Masters Degrees & Graduate Certificates, plus technical education certificates in Interactive Multimedia),

(b.) Police (Diploma of Criminal Investigation at the Police Academy, General Investigators Course, Specialist Courses and Detective School), and

(c.) Industry Courses (Microsoft Cert Sys Engineer, A+ Hands On & Computer Professional, Compumatics Cert. Comp Engineer – RS101).

Respondent practitioners on average had attended 3 additional educational programs which ranged in duration from 30 days to 3 years equivalent full time study with an average duration being of greater than 1 year equivalent full time study. The educational programs undertaken are presented by order of popularity in Table 2. showing the programs attended by the most practitioners as being the most popular.

Table 2. Educational Programs Attended in Order of Popularity.

1	Police Academy Programs
2	Bachelor Science (Computer Science)
3	Master Science (Computer Security)
4	Graduate Diploma (Computer Science)
5	Graduate Certificate: Information Security
6	Microsoft Certified Systems Engineer
7	A+ Programs

Question 3 asked, "How have these training and educational programs assisted you in computer forensic and digital data evidence analysis?" Respondent practitioners identified a few similar core benefits that each expressed differently and may be categorized into three areas; Knowledge = 50%, Skills =30% and Leadership = 20%.

The final question in this section asked, "Given the opportunity, what training or educational courses would you undertake that directly relate to computer forensic and digital data evidence analysis?"

100% of respondent practitioners stated a desire to continue engagement in life long learning by attending education and training programs specifying only two of the three types of education programs previously identified: (a.) University (Masters Degrees and Graduate Certificates - shorter & more responsive to needs), and (b.) Industry Courses (advanced vendor training programs, file system programs, A+ Programs, IACIA CF Certification & ENCE). The omission of police courses may be because they address general rather than the specific needs of the respondent practitioners. The educational programs in order of popularity were; (1.) Specialist Advanced Forensic Tool Vendor Training, (2.) Advanced Industry recognised Vendor Programs, (3.) Graduate Certificate (Computer Science), and (4.) Master Science (Internet Security). The respondent practitioners identified only two areas as being beneficial for future training and education; Knowledge = 15%, with a concerted emphasis on Skills = 85%.

From the answers given to these questions one may concur that;

(a)   practitioners have demonstrated their willingness to engage in both education programs and training courses,

(b)   university programs are desirable,

(c)   respondent practitioners consider skills orientated programs as mo st desirable.

It would appear that an ideal solution is to integrate academic courses with a strong theory and conceptual base together with the skills to apply these concepts in practice.

4 Conclusions

Based on the analysis of collected data, one may conclude that respondent practitioners have a strong desire to engage in educational and training programs with an emphasis on gaining firstly practical skills and secondly recognition that accompanies academic qualification. This could be construed to suggest practitioners want the best of two worlds. One world providing the best of practical skills combined with the other world providing academic recognition and where the combination of both worlds offers the perception of better personal integrity to the practitioners.

The acquisition of immediate skills without the opportunity for engagement of thought and time for contemplation builds a capacity that is without a solid theory base and only able to address aspects within its immediate skill set before jeopardizing the practitioner's integrity. Addressing skills only is a short term solution to a long term problem. Academia needs to teach concepts and how to apply them rather than focus on the sales of skills and particular products. The respondent practitioners however, hold as primary importance getting the job done successfully. There is evidence that practitioners on occasion engage in tasks or on work which is undertaken on the basis of trial and error, and conferring with fellow practitioners seeking particular advice when necessary because there is little academic support readily available that is of practical value to the given situation. Vendors attempt to provide single forensic workbench tool as an ultimate solution. Academic rigour requires a period of contemplation time not conducive to maintaining education programs with skills required by respondent practitioners to be readily available today. Both universities and vendors have a duty to continue striving to support practitioners by engaging and working together.

References

1. Armstrong, C. J., 2003. *Developing A Framework for Evaluating Computer Forensic Tools*. Australian Institute of Criminology Conference, Canberra ACT, Australia.
2. Armstrong, C. J., 2003, Mastering Computer Forensics, in *Security Education and Critical Infrastructures*, Irvine, Cynthia and Armstrong, Helen, (Ed's), Kluwer Academic Publishers, Boston, pp 151-158
3. Armstrong, C. J., 2005, *Development of a Research Framework for Selecting Computer Forensic Tools*. Masters Thesis, Curtin University of Technology, Perth, Western Australia.
4. Armstrong, H. and Forde, P., 2003, Cyber criminals and their use of the Internet, *Journal of Information Management & Computer Security*, October, Vol. 11, No. 5.
5. Armstrong, H. and Russo, P., 2004, *Electronic Forensics Education Needs of Law Enforcement*. Conference Proceedings of CISSE8 2004, United States Military Academy, West Point, NY June 2004
6. Armstrong, H. and Russo, P., 2005, *Walking the Beat on the path to technology, Developing computer savvy Police*. Conference Proceedings of WISE4 – 4th World Conference on Information Security Education, May 18-20, Moscow, Russia
7. Armstrong, C. and Jayaratna, N., 2004. *Teaching Computer Forensics: Uniting Practice with Intellect*. CISSE8, United States Military Academy, West Point, NY
8. Broersma, M, 2004, *UK Internet Crime Efforts are Criminal says Study*, Computerworld (Sunday, 23 May 2004), Available on-line @ WWW: http://www.computerworld.co.nz/news.nsf/UNID/BB017D2244CD06D3CC256E9 A0073384A
9. EURIM, 2004, *Supplying the Skills for Justice*, Available on-line @ WWW: http://www.eurim.org/consult/ecrime/may_04/ECS_DP3_Skills_040 505_web.htm
10. Jayaratna, N. 1999, *Understanding and Evaluating Methodologies. NIMSAD : A Systemic Framework*, McGraw-Hill Book Company, Maidenhead.
11. Kruse Warren G. & Heiser Jay G., 2002, *Computer Forensics: Incident Response Essentials*, Addison-Wesley, Boston
12. Littlejohn Shinder Debra, and Tittel Ed, 2002, *Scene of the Cybercrime: Computer Forensics Handbook*, Syngress
13. Roast, S., Lavender, P. and Wisniewski, T., 2001, Global Impacts, Future Challenges and Current Issues in training within the Police Computer Crime Unit, *Proceedings of the Second World Conference on Information Security Education*, July, Western Australia, pp 7-23
14. Slade Robert, 2004, *Software Forensics: Collecting evidence from the scene of a digital crime*, McGraw-Hill
15. Vatis, M. A., 2002. *Law Enforcement Tools and Technologies for Investigating Cyber Attacks. A National Needs Assessment*. Hanover, NH, Institute for Security Technology Studies at Dartmouth College.
16. Warren, M., 2003, Australia's Agenda for E-security Education and Research, in *Security Education and Critical Infrastructures*, Irvine, Cynthia and Armstrong, Helen, (Ed's), Kluwer Academic Publishers, Boston, pp 109-114

Resubmit my Information Security Thesis? – You must be joking!

Helen Armstrong, Louise Ynström

[1] School IS, Curtin University, Hayman Road, Bentley, Western Australia
[2] Department Computer & System Sciences, DSV, Kista, Stockholm, Sweden
[1] H.Armstrong@.curtin.edu.au
[2] Louise@dsv.su.se

Abstract. This paper presents a model for use by students and supervisors embarking upon higher degrees by research with specific application to information security. The model details a set of questions to be asked in preparing for the research in order to ensure a well planned and cohesive research project and written thesis.

Keywords: Higher degrees by research, information security education, research supervision, examination of higher degrees by research.

1   Introduction

In the supervision and examination of students undertaking higher degrees by research in information security it has been the observation of numerous authors that many students and supervisors miss crucial aspects in the research planning and progression, thus jeopardizing the examination outcome. In their research on doctoral theses examination Mullins and Kiley [1] comment that poor theses were characterized by lack of coherence, lack of understanding of the theory, lack of confidence, researching the wrong problem, mixed or confused theoretical and methodological perspectives, work that is not original, and not being able to explain what had actually been argued in the thesis.

An analysis by the authors of 10 higher degree by research theses in the final stages - pre-examination or examination – indicates all had major shortcomings requiring rewriting or resubmission. An analysis of shortcomings in the 10 theses examined over the recent past has highlighted the following problems:

1. Scope is not clearly delineated, and students become sidetracked.
2. Aims are not clearly detailed, and the end product of the research is not defined.
3. Significance of the theoretical research contribution is poorly supported.
4. Research involving physical artifacts or application developments are not abstracted to provide a contribution to theory.
5. Theoretical base of the research is unclear, or theory presented in isolation with no clear integration to the rest of the research.
6. Significant amount of irrelevant material included in the literature reviews.
7. Omission of important past research in the area.

Please use the following format when citing this chapter:

Armstrong, H., Ynström, L., 2007, in IFIP International Federation for Information Processing, Volume 237, Fifth World Conference on Information Security Education, eds. Futcher, L., Dodge, R., (Boston: Springer), pp. 9–16.

8. Large number of sources presented in the literature review lacking academic rigor.
9. Literature discussion does not indicate a need for the current research.
10. Research method discussed but not fully understood, and the appropriateness of the chosen research method not justified.
11. Incorrect usage of basic academic research concepts, i.e. system, methodology, model, framework, ontology, paradigm, taxonomy, etc.
12. Aspects of validity and reliability of data collection instruments poorly handled.
13. Integration of the research lacking with obvious links missing, lack of cohesion in the research as a whole.
14. Lack of focus regarding where this research fits in the field, i.e. past, present and future research.

The field of information security is young and interdisciplinary, handling contemporary problems of wide varieties. It asks students to link future knowledge, applications, mechanisms, procedures and the like to the historical anticipation of a strong and ongoing evolution which is different in breadth and depth to the pure sciences. Supervisors of information security research students need to ensure their students have perspicuity and clearly understand what they are expected to produce and how. The recurrence of similar shortcomings to those listed above in numerous theses has led the authors to believe a discussion of considerations common in thesis examination would be beneficial for information security research students and supervisors in not only planning and carrying out research, but also determining whether a thesis is ready for examination. The authors are aware of many different forms of editing a thesis; ranging from a paper collection with an introduction showing how the different papers contribute to a wholeness, and a monograph where chapters are designed to altogether present a coherent wholeness. Nevertheless, the examiners' questions presented are equally valid for any editorial form.

2   Areas for Consideration

The questions an examiner asks when assessing a higher degree by research thesis are similar across the globe. One of the first tasks of the examiner is to gain an understanding of the research in its entirety, as a holistic piece of work. A scan of the contents and the abstract should explain what was done, why it is important, how it was done and how it all fits together into the bigger picture. The examiner then looks at the contents in more detail.

In particular, examiners of higher degrees by research theses look for the following essential elements (in addition to other characteristics) [1] [2] [3] [4] [5]:
1. A significant contribution to theoretical knowledge - new knowledge in information security must be presented.
2. A sound understanding of research methodologies and employment of a research methodology and design appropriate to the information security research being undertaken.

3. An in-depth review of literature and analyses of past research in the specific area of information security covered.

4. Depth, clarity, integration and cohesion of the research as a holistic venture in information security as reflected in the thesis.

If the thesis does not include the above elements to an acceptable level then it is highly likely that the student will be required to resubmit. Unfortunately the PhD examination process differs across the international spectrum disadvantaging those who have to publish their written thesis before the final examination. Theses may be 'failed' if one or more of the above crucial factors is not met and the examiners consider there is no way the thesis can be raised to the required standard. [2]

Ensuring a piece of research (as reflected in the thesis) meets the above requirements is a wise undertaking as early as possible in the research process and advantages abound for those who plan their research projects with these elements in mind. By taking on the mindset of an examiner students and their supervisors can check that the research fulfils the examiners' expectations as the research progresses, rather than waiting until the research is nearly complete, when much reworking may need to be done before submission.

The following sections explain the questions an examiner will ask when they consider an information security research thesis for assessment. Considering these questions and addressing these requirements early in the research will ensure a well planned and executed piece of research, resulting in a much more rewarding experience for not only the student and supervisors, but also the subsequent examiners.

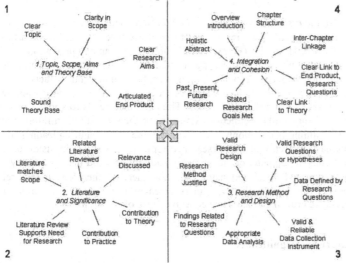

Fig. 1: Areas higher degree by research theses examiners will consider categorized into four quadrants.

Figure 1 shows the areas an examiner will consider categorized into four sections as reflected in the four quadrants in the diagram: 1-Focus of the research including topic, scope, aims and theory base, 2- Past research and magnitude of the contribution covering literature and significance, 3- Research process and findings covering research methodology and design, and 4- Holistic appreciation of the research centering on integration and cohesion. The four quadrants do not stand alone but integrate closely as denoted by the four-way arrow in the centre of the diagram.

2.1   Topic, Scope, Aims and Theory Base

Definition of the topic area and scope provides a boundary via which the breadth and depth of the research can be discussed.   The focus of the research with relation to base theoretical concepts and the aims to be achieved are key considerations by examiners.

Question: Is the topic area clear and well-scoped? The examiner looks to see if the topic area and scope of the research is well defined and articulated. Many topic areas in information security overlap with others and it is helpful to define not only what is included in the research, but also what is excluded. Many students spend valuable time investigating and considering irrelevant topics and tools (such as cognitive maps, rich pictures, storyboards, Venn diagrams, network diagrams, flow diagrams, and matrices) for defining the areas for inclusion should be used early in the research. However, at the commencement of an investigative research project there may also be areas which do not clearly fall inside or outside, but remain in a grey area until the research is further advanced. The research topic may need to be honed as the project progresses.

Question: Are the research aims clear and achievable? Has the end product of the research been articulated? The aim or objectives of the research need to be articulated early in the written thesis. The research should produce an end product in a conceptual, logical and/or physical form. Typical end products of research in information security include models, methodologies, frameworks, taxonomies and artifacts.

Question: Does the research have a sound theory base? Academically sound research needs to have a solid theoretical base. The examiner needs to know if the research involves theory building, theory extension, or theory testing. In information security theory building is commonly used for new topic areas featuring leading edge concepts, whereas research into well-researched topic areas such as intrusion detection systems, trends in computer crime, authentication models and the like usually involve theory testing and theory extension. The examiner will then look for the relationships between the chosen theory, the research process and the research end product as these are crucial elements to a cohesive piece of research.

2.2   Literature and Significance

Every examinable piece of research submitted for a higher degree by research must make a significant contribution to the body of knowledge. This contribution must be new and unique, so it is crucial to ensure you are not duplicating work others may have completed in the past.

Question: Does the structure and content of literature review match the scope? Is the literature reviewed directly related to the research and is the relevance of the lit-

erature discussed? The scope of the research commonly forms the boundary for the literature review. The literature review should contain only topics which are directly related to the research in question. Examiners will look for evidence of analysis of past work in the area, not just a summary of what has been written on the topic. The relevance of each topic to the current research should also be stated.

Question: Does the literature discussion support the need for the research? The literature review should culminate in a discussion which draws out the main points from the review and justifies the current research. This is a crucial element of the thesis ensuring the need for the research is clearly indicated, based firmly upon research in the area in the past.

Question: Is the contribution to theory (and practice, if applicable) significant and clear? It is important that the researcher has clarified the contribution made and presented this clearly for the examiner to see. The main contribution sought is one of academic knowledge via a conceptual construction, i.e. adding to theoretical or conceptual knowledge in some form, such as a theory or a model. If the research focus is more practical, then this conceptual contribution can be synthesized into a practical contribution, such as a set of guidelines or standards, or an evaluation matrix or the like.

2.3   Research Method and Design

The examiner needs to be convinced that an appropriate research method and design has been applied.

Question: Is the chosen research method appropriate and well-justified? The examiner will seek to ensure the student has demonstrated they have a sound understanding of research methodologies and have articulated why the chosen methodology is relevant. The examiner will also look to ensure the terminology is correct – for example if you claim to be developing a framework for comparing digital forensics tools, ensure you have built a static higher level model which provides a structure to help connect the set of computer forensics concepts or aspects researched.

Question: Is the research design valid? Describe the research process in detail explaining the reasons for undertaking the steps detailed in the research design.

Question: Are the research questions or hypotheses valid and appropriate? The research should focus upon researching an area in order to answer specific questions about that area which will lead to an increase in knowledge about that field. The examiner will look to see that appropriate questions have been asked and valid hypotheses raised. The null hypothesis H_1 should be the expected result, that is, the fallback position when hypothesis H_0 is not found to be proven true.

Question: Is the data collected defined by the research questions? Many research projects collect data which is superfluous to the stated research objectives. The research questions (or hypotheses) need to guide the data collected and ensure only necessary analyses of data is carried out. For each research question it is helpful to ask: what data is needed, what is the source of this data, where can it be found, when is the most appropriate time to collect this data, what is the most effective instrument to use, what sample size is necessary to achieve reliable and valid results. A simple tool for this purpose is illustrated in Table 1.

Table 1: A suggested layout for defining data requirements

Research Question (Why)	Data Needed (What)	Source of Data (Who)	Location (Where)	Timing (When)	Instrument (How)	Number Needed (How Many)
1.						
2.						

Question: How valid and reliable are the data collection instruments? How appropriate are the data analysis methods chosen? The examiner will ensure level of external validity is appropriate for the claimed generalizability of the findings. Any trace of bias evident in data collection and analyses will be reported back to the student. The measures taken to ensure reliability and validity need to be clearly presented. In information security projects triangulation of data and method are common methods used to increase validity. Particular notice will be taken by the examiner of the appropriateness of the criteria and measures, the application of statistical or data analysis methods, and the use of instrument testing and pilot projects.

Question: Are the findings from the research related to the research questions? Each of the research questions must be answered and the process of obtaining the findings must be plainly delineated. In many cases students have difficulty organizing their findings as the results from investigation often reveal more than answers to the specific research questions posed. The findings would then need to be separated so that answers to the research questions are differentiated from other findings discussed.

2.4   Integration and Cohesion

This section deals with the structure and integration of the written thesis as a whole piece of work, and in the experience of the authors this is the most difficult area for research students to achieve.

Question: Does the abstract encapsulate the project in its entirety? The abstract needs to succinctly describe the research project, explaining what it aims to achieve and why it is important. An overview of the research approach should also be included, explaining at a high level the analysis undertaken and the results found.

Question: How succinctly does the introduction set the scene? The introduction is an opportunity to set the scene and give the required background to the research. Many students erroneously believe they must start at the beginning and give a detailed history of information security. The readers of a thesis are usually other researchers in the area, and an extended discussion of irrelevant materials easily frustrates examiners and knowledgeable readers. Design the introduction wisely – use it to set the scene and give information that is essential to understanding the rest of the thesis.

Question: How well are chapters structured and linked? Each chapter of the thesis needs to tell one part of the story, and all the chapters should link to form one coherent story rather than a series of isolated short stories. Ensure the chapters are well-structured, paragraph and sentence structure is correct and the chapters are connected. If you have a paper collection, the 'coat' chapter/s should equally compactly link each separate paper's contribution to the scope and aims of the coherent big story, leaving details to the specific papers.

Question: Do chapter conclusions link to theory base, end product and research questions? The conclusion of each chapter should discuss how the content of that chapter is linked to the theory, end product and/or research questions. There should be a clear pathway through all parts of the thesis towards the end goal. At the end of the research the examiner will ask 'what effect did the findings of the research have on the theory?'

Question: How well have the research goals been met and is there critical reflection? The examiner will be evaluating how well you have achieved the aims or goals stated earlier in your thesis. An over-inflated statement of aims may result in the examiner concluding the objectives have not been fully met. The actions to progress towards achieving the aims are a key aspect under examination, and should be transparent to the examiner. Examiners also look for critical reflection by the student of their own work [1] [3].

Question: How clear is the context of this research – past, present and future? The examiner will look to see if there is continuity in the research, that the current research has been placed in context and that there are areas into which this research may be extended. It is helpful to compare the findings of the current research with the findings of past research, most of which should have been covered in the literature review. Areas of future research are important and these will usually link to areas outside the specific scope of the research under examination.

3   Summary

Shortcomings in theses for students enrolled in higher degrees by research relating to information security have been a more frequent occurrence in the experience of the authors. Guidance relating to the expectations of examiners given to these students appears to be insufficient, commonly resulting in a resubmission requirement or a fail grade.

The field of information security is generally young and our researchers do not have the same wealth of experience in research to draw from in comparison to the pure sciences. The race against time is always present in information security in order to share the new knowledge, particularly as researchers in this field battle to keep up with the pace of technological progress and criminal activity. Ideally every student works towards a successful result from examination of their thesis, and the areas considered by examiners of information security theses discussed in this paper provide a valuable set of questions students and supervisors can ask of the research thesis before it is submitted for examination. A summary of the questions discussed above appears in Table 2.

Table 2: A summary of the examiners' questions

Area	Questions
Topic, Scope, Aims and Theory Base	Is the topic area and scope clearly defined?
	Are the research aims clear and achievable?
	Has the end product of the research been articulated?
	Does the research have a sound theory base?
Literature and Significance	Does the structure and content of literature review match the scope?
	Is the literature reviewed directly related to the research?
	Is the relevance of the literature discussed?
	Does the literature discussion support the need for the research?
	Is the contribution to theory significant and clear?
	Is the contribution to practice significant and clear (if applicable)?
Research Method and Design	Is the chosen research method appropriate and well-justified?
	Is the research design valid?
	Are the research questions or hypotheses valid?
	Is the data collected defined by the research questions?
	How valid and reliable are the data collection instruments?
	How appropriate are the data analysis methods chosen?
	Are the findings from the research related to the research questions?
Integration and Cohesion	Does the abstract encapsulate the project in its entirety?
	How succinctly does the introduction set the scene?
	How well are chapters structured and linked?
	Do chapter conclusions link to theory base, research questions and end product?
	How well have the research goals been met and is there critical reflection?
	How clear is the context of this research – past, present and future?

Although the focus of this paper is on research predominantly in the field of information security, the model presented could be easily extrapolated into other related areas.

References

1. Mullins, Gerry & Kiley, Margaret, 2002, "It's a PhD, not a Nobel Prize': how experienced examiners assess research theses", Studies in Higher Education, Vol 27, No. 4, pages 369-386
2. Johnston, Sue, 1997, "Examining the Examiners: an analysis of examiners' reports on doctoral theses", Studies in Higher Education, Vol. 22, No. 3, pages 333-347
3. Holbrook Allyson, Bourke Sid, Loval Terence & Dally Kerry, 2004, "Investigating PhD thesis examination reports", International Journal of Educational Research, Vol 41, pages 98-120
4. Keen, Peter G.W.: "Relevance, and Rigor in Information Systems Research: Improving Quality, Confidence, Cohesion and Impact", in Nissen, H-E et al. (Eds) Information Systems Research: Contemporary Approaches and Emergent Traditions, Elsevier Science Publishers B.B. (North-Holland) IFIP 1991, pp 27 – 49
5. Smith, Alan Jay, "The Task of the Referee", 0018-9162/90/0400-0065501-00, 1990 IEEE

E-Voting as a Teaching Tool

Matt Bishop

Department of Computer Science
University of California, Davis
bishop@cs.ucdavis.edu

Abstract. Electronic voting systems are widely used in elections. This paper describes using an e-voting system as the basis for a project in an undergraduate computer security class. The goal of the project was to teach the students how to use the Flaw Hypothesis Methodology to perform a penetration study.

Keywords: computer security, information assurance, electronic voting, flaw hypothesis methodology, penetration study

1 Introduction

The mark of a good class is that the topic becomes more than an abstraction. The students are able to translate their knowledge into something tangible, and to apply what they learn in real life. Computer security offers many opportunities to do this. One of the most exciting applications is to electronic voting.

Electronic voting is particularly well suited for an introductory class in computer security. The act of voting is a process that most students are familiar with, and that many have done. But "electronic voting" or, more precisely, the use of electronic voting systems (called "e-voting systems" here), is simply a small part of how elections are run. Elections involve many processes and procedures, including designing ballots, reporting results, managing the precincts and polling stations, and so forth. E-voting systems are designed to replace paper ballots. The theory is that eliminating paper will cut storage costs, make discerning the voter's intent simpler by eliminating ambiguity in marks or "hanging chad", and allow automated counting of votes so that results can be reported more quickly.

The numerous reports of problems with e-voting systems in the media raise questions about the utility, accessibility, and security of these systems. Yolo County uses "optical scanning," in which voters mark paper ballots that are then scanned to count the votes. In order to meet the accessibility requirements of the Help America Vote Act, the Clerk-Recorder used Hart InterCivic DAU eSlate systems, chosen in part because the optical scanning systems were from Hart InterCivic, and in part because they were the most responsive and easiest of the e-voting vendors to work with. The Clerk-Recorder asked if we could have our students examine the systems and report on any specific policies and procedures that should be in place in order to protect the use of the systems—in less precise terms, what did she need to do to keep them secure?

Please use the following format when citing this chapter:

Bishop, M., 2007, in IFIP International Federation for Information Processing, Volume 237, Fifth World Conference on Information Security Education, eds. Futcher, L., Dodge, R., (Boston: Springer), pp. 17–24.

Section 2 describes some necessary background, specifically the flaw hypothesis methodology and some details about how elections are run. Section 3 describes the structure of the project, and section 4 the results of the exercise. The paper concludes with some thoughts on the exercise.

2   Background

We begin with a review of the flaw hypothesis methodology, and then describe how an election in Yolo County works.

2.1   The Flaw Hypothesis Methodology

The flaw hypothesis methodology [1] is a structured technique for performing penetration studies. It is most effective when done in the environment in which the system is to be used; then policies and procedures will affect the results, either for better or for worse.

The methodology consists of four phases.

1. In the *information gathering* phase, the testers analyze the environment and the system to learn as much about both as they can. They learn how the system is deployed, operated, and shut down. They learn about the stated policies and procedures, and how those are actually practiced.
2. Using the knowledge and information obtained from the first phase, the testers then *hypothesize flaws* in the system. They may also draw on their knowledge of related systems, and of the flaws in those systems. Human failings are a valuable source of flaws, because people often do not follow proper procedures—or the procedures for handling unexpected or rare events may not exist.
3. The third phase *tests the hypothesized flaws*. Often, time limits or other constraints prevent all the hypotheses from being tested. Those that are must be documented thoroughly. If the test demonstrates that the flaw does not exist, the testers proceed to the next flaw. But if the flaw does exist, the testers proceed to the next phase.
4. The final phase is *generalization*. In this phase, the testers examine the flaws they have found, and try to generalize them to find other flaws. As an example, if 3 network daemons have similar flaws, a logical generalization is that a library common to all 3 daemons contains a flaw.

We have used this methodology in projects in the past. One class helped test an intrusion tolerant system. The system specification stated that the system's performance would degrade no more than 25% if an attacker gained access to it. Therefore, the goal of the penetration test was to gain unauthorized access to the system and then cause a degradation of system performance by more than 25%. A different class tested a deception mechanism; the goal of the study was to determine the type of system being targeted. In both cases, we used special control mechanisms to restrict the students so they would not accidentally attack systems other than those involved in the test. For the voting machines, we kept the systems in locked rooms, and did not connect them to any networks. All access required the students to be physically present. This simulated the environment in which the machines would be used, as California forbids them to be connected to a network.

2.2 Elections and All That

Elections have several security-related requirements. Key ones are *accuracy* (the votes are recorded and counted accurately), *anonymity* (no ballot can be associated with a particular voter; this is sometimes called *secrecy of the ballot*), and *secrecy* (no voter can prove how he or she voted to a third party; this prevents selling of votes). California imposes other specific requirements for elections. For example, every e-voting system in California must provide a paper trail that the voter can use to verify his or her vote is recorded correctly. This *Voter-Verified Paper Audit Trail* (VVPAT) is used in recounts and is the official record of votes. In addition, only voting systems that the Secretary of State has certified may be used. The certification process examines both hardware and software. This bans the downloading of last-minute "bug fixes" or enhancements.

Unlike many other e-voting systems, the eSlate is not a self-contained unit. A cable connects each eSlate to a second device, called a *Judge's Booth Controller* or JBC. The eSlates may be daisy-chained, up to 12 per JBC. However, in Yolo County, each JBC has one eSlate because only one eSlate would be present at each polling location. The extra cable, coming out of the eSlate and intended to be connected to another eSlate, is tucked into a compartment at the top of the voting unit under a hood called the *privacy hood*. This hood hides the voter as he or she used the eSlate, so observers cannot tell how the voter votes.

When a voter is to vote using the eSlate, a poll worker uses the JBC to generate a 4-digit access code. The voter enters this code into the eSlate. The eSlate notifies the JBC, and the JBC records the access code as used, so it cannot be reused. The voter is then presented with the appropriate ballot, and votes. At the end of the session, the voter is given a summary showing how the votes were recorded, and the summary is printed on a reel of paper in a printer seated in the unit. If the voter accepts the ballot, he or she presses a button to cast the ballot. The VVPAT is marked accordingly, and the eSlate informs the voter that the ballot has been cast. If the voter rejects the ballot, the paper summary is marked as having been rejected, and the voting process restarts.

The vote is stored both on the eSlate and on the JBC. When recounts are performed, the VVPAT and not the electronic record is used.

3 The Project

ECS 153, "Computer Security", is an undergraduate course that introduces computer security to majors in computer science. Students from other technical disciplines also often take it. The class covers the basic principles, models, and concepts of computer security and assurance.

A major component of the course is a term-long project, sometimes individual, sometimes a class project, in which students apply many of the principles, methodologies, and technologies discussed in the class. This term, the project was to examine the e-voting system to be used by Yolo County and suggest policies and procedures necessary to ensure that the system works properly. We intended the students to gain a deeper understanding of how to apply the flaw hypothesis methodology, to learn about "black box testing," and to discover how a seemingly simple set of requirements requires a complex balance of technology and procedures to implement a particular task—voting. At no time did we have access to source code, or to the ballot generation or tallying systems.

3.1   Phase 1: Information Gathering

Because security depends upon environment, especially when the environment defines the function of the system (as is true with voting), the students needed to learn some details about how voting works. Further, they had to understand how an e-voting system fit within the context of an election. So, the information gathering phase had to include not just the system but also the environment.

The first step of this phase was to determine what an e-voting system should do in an election held in Yolo County. Their report had to list the requirements for an election and explain whether meeting each requirement would involve the e-voting system. For example, one requirement is that only registered voters vote. The e-voting system, which records and tallies votes, is not involved here because only registered voters can use the e-voting system[1]. A second requirement is that the votes be tallied accurately. The e-voting system is intimately involved with this requirement, because it tallies the votes cast on it.

All students knew an election was supposed to produce a winner or winners, and that how someone voted was to be secret. Few realized the problem of votes being sold, which was one of the major objections to paper trails[2]. So the first step was for the students to do research and brainstorm about what the requirements for an election were.

The second step built on the first. Given the set of requirements, if an e-voting system were to be used, which requirements would be applicable to the system? As an example, the requirement of accuracy is clearly applicable because if the machine misrecords votes, then the results of the election will be inaccurate. But the requirement that the systems be delivered to the polling places on time is not a requirement that affects the e-voting systems; it is instead an organizational requirement under the control of people.

So, the first report for the project had two distinct elements. First, the students had to enumerate a set of requirements for the election, and justify them.

---

[1] California does not allow provisional ballots to be cast electronically.

[2] All paper trails are protected so the voter cannot take a record of his or her votes away from the machine.

Second, the students had to examine each requirement to determine whether an e-voting system would affect whether that requirement was met.

3.2   Phase 2: Flaw Hypothesis Generation

In this phase, the students thought of possible flaws in the use of the e-voting systems. They used the results of the first phase as the basis for this work. The students examined the requirements relevant to e-voting systems, and developed a set of threats which, if realized, would prevent the requirements from being satisfied. The teams read reports about threat modeling of elections [2, 3]. and earlier studies of electronic voting systems to get ideas [4–9].

During this step, the Yolo County Clerk-Recorder's office gave a demonstration of how the eSlate system worked. This helped the students understand what the system looked like and how it would be used. They also learned how the systems were stored, how they would be distributed, and how the results would be brought back to the county seat and counted.

3.3   Phase 3: Flaw Hypothesis Testing

In the next phase, the students had to develop tests that confirmed or refuted their hypotheses. This required the students to analyze the threats, develop general hypotheses, and then refine them to make them testable.

As an example, one good "high-level" hypothesis was that a voter could vote on the eSlate without authorization from the JBC. But there are many ways to vote on an eSlate without authorization from the JBC. One could look at the access code generated by the poll worker, and quickly enter the booth and use the code before the one to whom the code was given. A bug in the software could allow any random 4-digit number to unlock the eSlate. Someone could guess an access code successfully. In order to test the hypothesis, a more specific hypothesis (or set of hypotheses) must be made.

In some cases, students would not be able to carry out the appropriate tests, particularly when the test required equipment that was not available. For example, one team suggested monitoring the electromagnetic emissions from the voting system to read the votes of the voter in the booth; but we did not have access to the necessary equipment. We encouraged the students to list all the tests they wanted to run, along with how to interpret the results of the tests.

For this exercise, the students were told to assume the attackers had unfettered access to the e-voting system. This meant that attacks such as the Princeton virus [10] or Hursti I and II [9] were fair game. With proper precautions, the likelihood of those attacks being successfully launched can be reduced to any desired probability. So, while unrealistic, this assumption set the stage for the last phase of the project.

3.4   Extra Phase: Remediation

A principle tenet of the way ECS 153 is taught holds that students must learn how to fix problems they find. Hence, they were asked to describe policies and procedures that would hinder or (ideally) prevent any attacks that exploited problems they found.

4   Results

The students were enthusiastic about the project (in part, one suspects, because of the election in the middle of the term). Some teams focused on physical flaws; others looked for problems relating to the software.

One set of hypotheses focused on disconnecting power or cables to see if the vote totals on the JBC, eSlate, and printed paper could differ. Teams focused on the connection between the printer and the eSlate unit. They tried unplugging the connection at various times in the voting proccess. For example:

Hypothesis: One can vote with the printer disconnected. If so, then one can cast a vote without a corresponding vote being recorded on the paper trail. This creates a discrepancy that will cause a vote not to be counted should a recount occur. The test was to disconnect the printer from the eSlate and then attempt to vote. The result was a failure; the eSlate would not accept an access code unless the printer were connected.

They also examined the connection between the eSlates and the JBC, and other eSlates. One team examined the daisy chaining of eSlates, and discovered that it was possible to reboot the JBC and all eSlates:

Hypothesis: The eSlate can be forced to use battery power throughout the election. Normally, the eSlate draws power from the serial cable connecting it to the JBC. It has an internal battery that is used should the power fail. One team noted that disconnecting the JBC's power, or tripping a switch in a conventional power strip, would have this effect. Another team found that plugging a DSUB-15 NULL terminator onto the end of the extra cable at the end of the daisy chain of eSlates caused the eSlates not to draw power from the JBC, thus running on battery power only. The difference in the attacks is instructive, because the first can be remediated by keeping power strips away from voters. The second is far more difficult to prevent, because a NULL terminator fits into a pocket, and the extra cable is concealed in a drawer under the privacy hood. It would take an observant poll worker to notice the motion of plugging the NULL terminator into the cable. The team suggested that the extra cable be removed to solve this problem. Indeed, the Clerk-Recorder has already requested permission to remove the extra cable, and the vendor agreed.

Some teams examined some software issues, trying to overflow buffers for write-in votes (which failed) or looking at the access codes to determine the difficulty of breaking the pseudo-random number generator:

Hypothesis: access codes can be predicted If access codes can be predicted, then at most one access code can be active at a time. So, for example, if a poll worker issued John an access code a_i, and Jane an access code a_{i+1}, then John can first vote with a_{i+1} (which he knows because he can predict the access code after his), and then vote with a_i. Several teams reported finding regularities in the sequences of access codes they examined, leading them to conclude the generator was not a cryptographically strong pseudo-random number generator.[3]

All teams concluded that proper policies and procedures would remediate the vulnerabilities they found. For the battery-draining flaw mentioned above, the recommended fix was to disconnect the extra cable. For the access code problem, the recommended fix was to ensure only one access code was active at any time. As stated earlier, in Yolo County, each polling station had only one eSlate. So, the recommended procedure was to issue one access code at a time. When the voter was done voting, the poll workers waited until he or she walked away from the eSlate before issuing the next access code.

Grading for the projects depended on the application of the methodology, and not on the number or type of flaws found. All the teams were very successful in the last two phases. Several teams had problems developing the requirements for an election; to help them, after the first phase, we provided a set of requirements that could be used in the second phase[4]. This "leveled the field", so to speak, so students who had trouble with the requirements could continue onto the next phase. Had this not been done, students on teams that did not develop an appropriate set of requirements would have been unable to develop the threats and meaningful hypotheses. With this common set of requirements, the teams all developed sets of threats that, while different, provided a firm basis for hypothesizing flaws.

5   Conclusion

The goal of this project was twofold. With respect to the class, the students were to learn how to perform a penetration study in a structured, methodical manner. This contrasts to the more popular approach of trying attack tools to see what works. That approach fails in the environment provided for the class, because e-voting systems are specialized systems with requirements not shared by most computers. Hence the students had to develop requirements and test against them in order to be able to determine whether they did, in fact, find flaws.

The second goal was to provide the Yolo County Clerk-Recorder with information about policies and procedures necessary to secure the systems on Election Day. Preliminary results were passed over before Election Day, which was halfway through the term. Interestingly, a number of students signed up to help deliver the eSlates and JBCs to polling places, and act as troubleshooters. To prepare them properly, the vendor arranged a troubleshooting class at UC Davis for the students (and others). The class was a success, everyone feeling that they better understood how the systems functioned and how to fix problems. Of course, this also led several students to hypothesize ways to attack should the recommended procedures not be followed.

---

[3] None, however, presented the algorithm used to derive the access codes.

[4] We did not say which ones affected the e-voting system, leaving that to the students.

As a result of their involvement in this project, several undergraduate students joined a group of graduate students who are analyzing the e-voting systems. This is an ongoing project, and one we hope will prove useful to Hart InterCivic, the Yolo County government, and ultimately the citizens of Yolo County who cast their vote, expecting it to be recorded and counted accurately.

Acknowledgments

The Yolo County Clerk-Recorder, Freddie Oakley, suggested this project and loaned us the electronic voting systems used in this study. She and Tom Stanionis readily provided information about how they planned to use the eSlates. Greg Hinson gave the class a demonstration of how the eSlates and JBCs were set up and used. Without their help, this project would have been impossible, and we thank them. We also thank Hart InterCivic for holding a troubleshooting class at UC Davis.

References

1. Linde, R.: Operating systems penetration. In: 1978 National Computer Conference, AFIPS Conference Proceedings. Volume 44. (1975) 361–368
2. Saltman, R.G.: Accuracy, integrity, and security in computerized vote-tallying. NBS Special Publication 500-158, Institute for Computer Sciences and Technology, National Bureau of Standards (now NIST), Gaithersburg, MD (August 1988)
3. Brennan Center Task Force on Voting System Security: The machinery of democracy: Protecting elections in an electronic world. Technical report, Brennan Center, 161 Avenue of the Americas, 12th Floor, New York, NY 10013 (August 2006)
4. Kohno, T., Stubblefield, A., Rubin, A.D., Wallach, D.S.: Analysis of an electronic voting system. In: Proceedings of the 2004 IEEE Symposium on Security and Privacy. (May 2004) 27–40 Appeared previously as Johns Hopkins University Information Security Institute Technical Report TR-2003-19, July 23, 2003.
5. Compuware Corporation: Direct recording electronic (DRE) technical security assessment report (November 2003) http://www.sos.state.oh.us/sos/hava/compuware112103.pdf.
6. Science Applications International Corporation: Risk assessment report: Diebold AccuVote-TS voting system and processes (September 2003) http://www.dbm.maryland.gov/SBE.
7. RABA Innovative Solution Cell: Trusted agent report: Diebold AccuVote-TS voting system (January 2004)
8. United States Computer Emergency Readiness Team: Diebold GEMS central tabulator vote database vote modification. Cyber Security Bulletin SB04-252 (September 2004) http://www.us-cert.gov/cas/bulletins/SB04-252.html.
9. Hursti, H.: Diebold TSx evaluation and security alert (May 2006) http://www.blackboxvoting.org/BBVtsxstudy.pdf.
10. Feldman, A., Halderman, J.A., Felten, E.: Security analysis of the Diebold AccuVote-TS voting machine. Technical report, Princeton University (September 2006)

Practical Assignments in IT Security for Contemporary Higher Education
An Experiment in Exploiting Student Initiative

Alan Davidson and Kjell Näckros

Department of Computer and Systems Sciences,
Stockholm University/Royal Institute of Technology, Sweden
{alan,kjellna}@dsv.su.se

Abstract. Modern university studies cater to large groups of students with consideable variation in background knowledge. This creates problems when designing viable practical exercises, not least for the subject of IT Security. We address these problems by creating a study environment within which students have the freedom to design and execute their own exercises. We suggest and test ideas for providing sufficient motivation and structure for student activity while minimising the need and cost for staff intervention.

Key words: IT Security, Practical Assignments, Pedagogics, Constructionist Learning

1 Introduction

Practical projects are of considerable pedagogical value for any learning environment, not least for university courses on IT Security. At the Department of Computer and Systems Sciences it has been our ambition to keep a practical element to our IT Security introductory courses, such as on the first, five week subject overview course of the Master's Programme in Information Security. During such courses we would like to tie several the more theoretical themes into a practical exercise. Since there is a lot of ground to cover in an overview course, and since most practical exercises concentrate on relatively narrow aspects of the subject, we do not believe it is motivated to spend more than one week's study time out of the five on practicals.

Some examples that were considered as candidates included red-team/blue team exercises and capture the flag competitions such as presented in [7], or the coding of buffer overflow exploits such as in [6]. There are however two main problems with this ambition:

1. Students who come to our courses have very mixed backgrounds. Though we have previously had many further educational students from industry, of late our subject matter has become far more popular with academic students. Neither of these groups can be expected to necessarily have, for example,

Please use the following format when citing this chapter:

Davidson, A., Näckros, K., 2007, in IFIP International Federation for Information Processing, Volume 237, Fifth World Conference on Information Security Education, eds. Futcher, L., Dodge, R., (Boston: Springer), pp. 25–32.

any knowledge of network protocols, computer architectures, programming, or any other operating system than Windows. We also have increasing numbers of international students, implying increased language difficulties and diversity in cultural background. All these factors combine and ultimatley make it very difficult to find any specific exercises that can stimulate all students - not without having to provide extensive background information and continuous assistance.

2. Practical experiments in IT Security are very sensitive to the computing environments used, and in the real world, these environments change rapidly. For example, for the buffer overflow exploit exercise mentioned above, after we had developed course material to illustrate the principle the linux kernel that ran on the student machines was routinely updated. There was no indication that address space randomisation had been included in the intervening kernel versions until our carefully designed exercise stopped working. Blue-team/red-team exercises will no doubt demand considerable upkeep if the systems, vulnerabilities, attacks and exploits are all to be kept realistically up to date.

If we are to keep our experiments relevant to the real world and thereby to our students, considerable resources will have to be spent in updating exercises, not to mention updating our practical knowledge in order to update the exercises. It should perhaps come as no surprise that we are not alone in experiencing such problems. To quote John Biggs:

> In the days when university classes contained highly selected students, enrolled in their faculty of choice, the traditional lecture and tutorial seemed to work well enough. However, the expansion, restructuring and refinancing of the tertiary sector that began in the 1990s has meant that classes are not only larger but quite diversified in terms of student ability, motivation and cultural background. Teachers have difficulty in just coping, let alone in maintaining standards, and are stressed. [1, p.1]

Modern texts on university pedagogics propose nothing short of an revolution in the organisation and financing structures in higher education in order to address such problems [3, 4]. While we are waiting for that revolution, we hope to make some headway by making the best of the situation.

2   What we have going for us

If we must play the hand we are dealt with, perhaps some of the cards are not too bad.

Modern Pedagogics - Researchers in the field of university pedagogics are encouraging us to cope with the diversity and the multitude of students in a number of ways. Diversity in students and in their learning processes can be addressed by flexibility in the learning environment. To quote Bowden and Marton in their book *The University of Learning*:

...students are more likely to adopt a deep approach to learning and are more likely to seek meaning and understanding if they are able to exercise a degree of choice about what and how they learn. It is important that, as much as possible, the learning environment is flexible so that students can exercise such choice and develop as the kind o independent learners we seek. [3, p.267]

In the same book the authors encourage us to shift from a view of our role as teachers to instead be facilitators of learning. This includes not only helping students to learn, but also always being open to learning from our students. This perhaps implies that the greater the number of students, the better are our opportunities to learn from them. To quote John Biggs again:

Effective teaching means setting up the teaching/learning context so that students are encouraged to react with the level of cognitive engagement that our objectives require. [1, p.56]

IT Security's Fascination - The field of IT Security is perhaps exceptional in that when it comes to its practical elements, most students are strongly self motivated. Having the knowledge of how to beat or break a system seems to have a particular allure. This might not be exactly the *level of cognitive engagement* that we require, but it is at least something to build upon.

Online Collaboration - The latest years have seen the rise of a new kind of social phenomenon on the Internet: Online collaboration and sharing. This phenomenon is so prevalent as to have been dubbed by some Web 2.0 [10]. The trend is evident in many forms, perhaps most notably in the emergence of *wikis* such as Wikipedia [9]. These are sites that contain an abundance of clearly structured information that has come about through the cooperation and general benevolence of Internet users. It is perhaps surprising that even though such a material could be easily vandalised or otherwise spoiled by just about anyone, it has been said to rival the accuracy of the Encyclopaedia Britannica [5]. This phenomenon could work for us in an academic context.

3   The Background

A dedicated IT Security laboratory has been in operation at the department since 2002. It embodies a switched sub-net which is separated from the rest of the department's computer networks by a highly restrictive firewall which in principle only allows http traffic to pass in and out of the subnet. This allows us to relax the security policy that the students are otherwise subject to when using the department network.

The main practical difference between exercises in a security laboratory and those conducted for other computer science courses is that for the most interesting experiments the students must be given, or allowed to acquire, system administrator privileges. This creates problems when the laboratories are shared among students, where each workstation is booked by a single student group for a number of hours at a time. If students are given administrator rights to a workstation they will have limitless possibilities to make that workstation unusable for the next group to use it, intentionally or not. What is more, it should be possible for a project to conducted and saved over several sessions without the risk of other students spoiling the environment for each other. This was solved by giving each workstation a removable hard-drive cassette as its bootable medium. Students are allowed to check out their own hard-drive cassette for the duration of their exercises. The workstations can net-boot under the control of the firewall server, giving the students the possibility to format their disk and to ghost clean images of operating systems to their disks. This environment has subsequently been christened The Sandbox. A number of exercises where devised for use in this environment. These exercises include experiments in Windows with system hardening, keylogging, spoofing, and using Trojan horses. In a linux system, they include experiments with system administration tools that allow for network sniffing, spoofing, vulnerability analysis, and intrusion detection. [2]

Due to the diversity of the students' technical experience there are no specific goals for each of these experiments. Instead, they are formulated as a number of steps that the student should follow and an exhortation that the student should observe and reflect upon what the see. Different students will have differing observational powers, but the idea is that no matter what the background of the student they should be able to make some sense out of what is happening and learn important lessons according to their own individual possibilities.

This was the basis for a one week's practical assignment for most of our introductory courses. Students worked in pairs and were required to hand in a written report where they not only should show that they had completed the assignment themselves, but they should also show evidence of how they had reflected upon their observations. They were exhorted to explicitly tie in their reflections to the theoretical framework that they studied in the course literature and at lectures. Students were not graded according to their results from this exercise (since they were working in pairs, and it is typical in Sweden not to give differential grades for cooperative projects) but given a pass or fail.

The results from these exercises was very varied. Many students reported that the Windows exercises were the most interesting and educational, although as these exercises were designed they are considerably more trivial than the linux based exercises. The linux based exercises were described in simple terms, but no doubt those students who had never before used linux were nevertheless intimidated by an interface so strange to them. Very few of the hand-ins were ever of a calibre that the exercise instructions called for. Reflections were seldom included, and only very vague links to the course material were made if at all. It was clear that students were interpreting the lack of clear goals as a licence to sub-optimize their efforts, and they were putting in far less than the expected 40hrs of laboratory time.

4 The Experiment

Goaded by the problems and encouraged by the possibilities as discussed above, we began a pedagogical experiment in 2005 where the students themselves suggest IT Security projects that they would like to work with. They are now first required to complete the exercise described above, but without the requirement of reflection; they simply have to document their experiments to show that they had completed it on their own. The first assignment now serves primarily as encouragement to get to know the laboratory and the basic tools. This assignment is expected to take no more than 16 hours of laboratory time.

The second part of the assignment, to design and execute an own experiment, should be designed to take 24 hours for each student. To this end they are allowed to form arbitrarily large groups as the experiment may require. No two separate groups are allowed to attempt the same project at the same time. Each project must be proposed in writing and approved by the course staff before work may progress. This is only a cursory process to make sure that the students themselves understand what they are embarking upon and that it is of suitable dimensions for the course. Since the projects are not overly vetted at the start, we spend greater effort on monitoring students' progress in the laboratory in order to catch any unforeseen problems at an early stage, and get the students quickly onto a more productive track.

The first time round, we gave a short list of suitable projects, just to get the ball rolling for those students who could not immediately design an own project:

- Install and test the usability of FreeBSD configured with Mandatory Access Control.
- Suggest a network usage profile (such as family network, or small company) and configure a firewall to suit that profile.
- We have a number of Security products made available to us from Computer Associates, including firewalls and intrusion detection software, together with tutorials. Install and evaluate one of these systems and their supplied course material.
- On the basis of advice on how to secure a system (as found at suitable sites on the Internet), secure the Windows 2000 and Linux systems on your hard drive, and compare the process for the two systems.
- Design exercises for Windows XP equivalent to (or preferably improved from) those you have done for Windows 2000.
- Install and configure a Honey Pot
- Install and test a Tar Pit
- Design a series of attacks for a chosen system configuration, e.g., for a certain version of Windows without all the latest safety packs.
- Install and test 2 different password checking programs.

This basic format was tested on our International Master's Programme in Computer Security two years in a row, 2004-2005. The results were encouraging in that many students could immediately find projects of their own liking. They generally spent more than the stipulated 24 hours per student on their projects, which although it might be considered detrimental to their other studies told us that this was promising from the motivational point of view.

5   Stage Two

Our ultimate ambition with these exercises has been to create a database of reusable security related experiments that students could pick and choose amongst as well as add to. This puts a greater demand on the final hand-in, i.e. the documentation, than would normally be required on such a course. We are more intent on the students learning a useful lesson from their experiment than worrying about finer details of its documentation. However, when students are running an experiment based on the documentation written by fellow students, whether finer details are included or not can mean the difference between effective learning and total frustration. If the course staff were responsible for checking the documentation in detail and requiring multiple complementary hand-ins until it reached the required level the whole process would become prohibitively costly.

As an alternative strategy we turned to the idea of wikis [8]. If the communal spirit can result in such a full and well structured material as the Wikipedia, we hope that the same could contribute to the gradual expansion, update and refinement of a student driven database of security exercises. In the Autumn term of 2006 we transferred some of the more interesting and better documented projects to a locally run wiki site. Students could now suggest their own projects by creating their own wiki page and submitting it for approval, or else they can choose an existing project from the wiki, mark it as booked, and then repeat the project with an aim to testing and improving its documentation.

We believe that some standardised formatting for these wiki pages must necessary be imposed to help the students to quickly decide on whether a project is of a suitable type and size to suit their level of abilities and their group size. As yet, it seems sufficient to impose a few standard header fields, such as project prerequisites and expected person hours to complete.

6   Preliminary Indications

Thus far we can say that our pedagogical experiment shows great promise. The database currently comprises of some 46 experiments, even if some are very close to another in their and one or two have been repeated in both Swedish and English with separate documentation. Initial worries that this strategy would result in chaos have proved to be unfounded. It seems that the students themselves are good judges of their own abilities and do not in general pick projects that get them into trouble. There is a proportion or projects that do fail to reach their original goal, but with expedient management from the course staff most of these worst effects have been avoided without it costing the students a great deal of frustration or the course staff a great deal of time.

At the time of writing, the second group of students to use wiki based documentation are deep into experimentation. The difference for this group compared to the previous ones is that they are heavily relying on texts written by previous students (sometimes foreign students with poor language skills in English) and it is already clear that they are developing an understanding of what is required of the documentation to make a project easily repeatable. A number of groups have expressed their prime goal to be to improve the documentation. As one of the explicit goal of the introductory course is that students should be able to communicate about IT Security after completing the course, this is a very positive result. It is, however, only relatively positive; we have found the level of ambition in the clarity and purpose of the documentation is mostly disappointing. Students are still largely motivated to show that they have done enough work for a pass, rather than to write the kind of documentation that they themselves would like to read.

In terms of learning from the students, this has been a very valuable project. From the course staff point of view many projects have turned out to be surprisingly easy. Some have been innovative. Some are surprisingly difficult, such as experiments in propagating worms and viruses, which have seldom worked. Without this eager student workforce the course staff would never have had the time to make the same discoveries.

We have for the most part been liberal and lenient in what projects we have allowed and what documentation we have passed. It has however been necessary to employ strict requirements in one particular aspect, i.e., ethics. Some projects have been suggested without due regard for the safety and security of the environment in which the experiment is to be conducted. This is despite considerable emphasis being put on issues of policy and ethics during the lecture series. Students who wish to conduct potentially dangerous experiments, such as building a simple virus or sniffing a wireless network, are required to give detailed specifications of the measures they will take to ensure that they minimise the risk to their environment. This at least is evidence that practical experiments are useful for driving home important lessons from the lectures, such as those on ethics, that are otherwise too easily missed.

7   The Future

A fuller evaluation of this experiment will be conducted after completion of the 2007 spring term course, where the normal student course evaluation will be augmented with more detailed questions on their experiences from the assignment. A thorough review of the current state of the experiment database will also be conducted. The preliminary results are however promising enough to suggest several ways to develop the ideas presented here.

The size and complexity of the current experiments has been limited by the 24hour per student limit. We would like to encourage more ambitious projects that can span a longer time period. This could be done once the exercises in the database have a stable enough core by the creation of a special course in practical experimentation. Students would be required to amass a number of hours and educational credits as related to the values in the experiment headers, to gain study credits.

We are enthusiastic to the idea of using virtual machines in order to prepare environments where the experiments are ready to run. It would also be very practical if one could run virtual machines as virtual security laboratories, thus liberating the student from the requirement to stay within the confines of our laboratory. We doubt however that these environments can be made secure enough to be confident that they will protect the systems they run within. Students should not have to become experts in the configuration and running of virtual machines in order to run security experiments.

A database of security experiments will invariably contain a certain amount of information that would be of interest to persons with ill intent. Though we hold the view that the experiments themselves are not malicious, and while we make every effort to ensure that our students use any knowledge gained for altruistic purposes only, it is a sensitive issue whether the department can or should make the database publicly available. For the sake of the material itself it would be most advantageous to allow the Internet in general to have access. Until that time, a happy compromise would be if we could establish cooperation between other schools of higher education so that such experiments could be shared. A network of secure VPN connections might also allow for the interconnection of similar security laboratories, which could open up exciting possibilities for not just shared experiments, but cooperative experiments.

References

1. Biggs, J.: Teaching for Quality Learning at University Open University Press, Slough, UK, 2003.
2. Blomquist, N., Nilsson, P., Peris, A.: Praktisk IT-säkerhetsutbildning - specifikation av utrustning, moment och administration, Master's Thesis No. 02-74. DSV, Stockholm University, 2002. In Swedish.
3. Bowden, J., Marton, F.: The University of Learning. RoutledgeFarmer, London, 1998.
4. Laurillard, D.: Rethinking University Teaching. Routledge, NY, 1993.
5. Nature: Internet encyclopaedias go head to head, March 2006, http://www.nature.com/news/2005/051212/full/438900a.html [visited 20070211]
6. Viega, J., McGraw, G.: Building Secure Software. Addison-Wesley 2002.
7. Vigna, G.: Teaching Network Security Through Live Exercises, in Proceedings of IFIP TC11/WG11.8 Third Annual World Conference on Information Security Education (WISE3), California, 2003.
8. wiki.org: What is Wiki?, http://www.wiki.org/wiki.cgi?WhatIsWiki, June 2002, [visited 20070211]
9. Wikipedia: http://www.wikipedia.org/ [visited 20070211]
10. Wikipedia: Web 2.0. http://en.wikipedia.org/wiki/Web_2 [visited 20070211]

Email Security Awareness – a Practical Assessment of Employee Behaviour

Hennie Kruger, Lynette Drevin, Tjaart Steyn
Computer Science & Information Systems
North-West University, Private Bag X6001, Potchefstroom, 2520
South Africa
Hennie.Kruger@nwu.ac.za, ldrevin@acm.org Tjaart.Steyn@nwu.ac.za

Abstract: Email communication is growing as a main method for individuals and organizations to communicate. Sadly, this is also an emerging means of conducting crime in the cyber world, e.g. identity theft, virus attacks etc. The need for improving awareness to these threats amongst employees is evident in media reports. Information security is as much a people issue as a technology one. This paper presents a description and results of an email awareness experiment that was performed amongst staff from a South African university. It is shown how management can use these results to focus and improve ICT awareness.

Keywords: Email security, identity theft, security awareness, employee behaviour

1   Introduction

The value of information in today's business environment has become increasingly important – information is regarded as an asset [1] and as such, is exposed to a wide variety of threats and vulnerabilities' that are usually addressed by a combination of technical and procedural controls. Technology and the associated technical solutions are necessary to address certain vulnerabilities such as viruses, denial of service attacks etc. However, information security is about more than technology; it also includes people. Dark [2] stated that the "people" piece of the security puzzle is perhaps the most critical. The lack of understanding security issues coupled with the pervasive and growing use of computers, makes people a critical factor in the information security equation.

One way to develop and motivate employees in an organisation to counter information security threats properly is through the implementation of security awareness programs. With appropriate knowledge, staff can better prevent information security breaches, detect malicious activities of other staff members and efficiently and effectively respond to security incidents [2]. To address information security awareness in an academic environment, a project was recently initiated to try and develop a measuring instrument for security awareness levels [3]. Key areas were identified to form the basis of the instrument and one of the key areas was the responsible use of email and the Internet. As part of the development of a measuring instrument it was also de-

Please use the following format when citing this chapter:

Kruger, H., Drevin, L., Steyn, T., 2007, in IFIP International Federation for Information Processing, Volume 237, Fifth World Conference on Information Security Education, eds. Futcher, L., Dodge, R., (Boston: Springer), pp. 33–40.

cided to make use of certain system data to evaluate users' behaviour in certain situations. To this end, four practical email tests were designed to test employees' awareness levels and behaviour when confronted with questionable email messages. The use of such practical tests has been used before. Dodge and Ferguson [4] described similar tests that were used to evaluate students' propensity to respond to email attacks.

The objective of this paper is to present a brief overview of the planning and execution of four email tests that were performed at a university to evaluate employees' behaviour. Results of the exercise will also be presented. The remainder of the paper is organised as follows: In section 2 the background to the exercise and the methodology used are discussed. Section 3 details the results of the four tests while section 4 presents some concluding remarks.

2   Background and Methodology used

2.1   Background

During 2006 a framework to evaluate ICT security awareness levels amongst employees was suggested [5]. The framework was based on the identification of key areas on which measurements can be taken. It was also suggested that, where appropriate, actual system generated data be used as measurements. System data is expected to be more reliable (not subjective) and fairly easy to obtain as opposed to data obtained by using questionnaires. One of the specific aspects that was identified as a key area to be measured and where system data could be useful to evaluate knowledge and behaviour, was the responsible use of the Internet and email facilities. The initial framework was developed at a university in an academic environment [3] and to obtain unbiased and objective data for this important area, four tests were designed to evaluate the same university's staff actions pertaining to certain email activities. All the tests were unannounced and distributed by means of email messages that requested staff to perform certain questionable actions – responses to these requests were then recorded and analysed. One of the tests aimed at identity theft, has already been described in detail in another article [6] but will be referred to again in this work for completeness sake.

As described in [6], the university where the tests were conducted is a South African university. The campus selected for the tests consists of eight divisions (academic faculties) and more than 26000 students. The campus is served by approximately 3400 staff members of whom about 550 are full-time academic staff. Although a high level of security is maintained, the university has no official security awareness program in place and staff did not receive any ICT security awareness training.

The design and execution of the four tests raised a number of issues to be solved before the actual tests could take place. Permission was obtained from senior management on the condition that no individual staff member would be identified during the exercise. Another aspect that needed careful planning was the content of the email messages. The messages had to be credible, not harming existing relationships and approved by the Manager Information Technology and the Human Resources department.

The design and motivation for the four tests can be summarized as follows:

Test 1 - The main idea was to send a questionable email to users and request them to click on a HTML link. The aim was to determine if users read and interpret what they receive and not automatically do what is requested. The message used in the email tried to convince users to follow a web link to obtain certain information that would be beneficial for their personal finances. The source of the email as well as the contents contained enough obvious questionable information to raise the suspicion of users and the correct, expected action of users should be to delete the message without following the link.

Test 2 - A questionable email was sent to users to try and trick them into opening a strange attachment with the objective of testing their reaction when confronted with attachments from an unknown source. The basic message was to invite users to get a free virus checker when clicking on the attachment and, as in test 1, the contents contained questionable information that should have caused users not to click on the attachment.

Test 3 - An email, that appeared to be legitimate, was sent to users, requesting them to follow a web link where they were asked to disclose private information (e.g. passwords) that could be used for identity theft. The aim was simply to gauge the reaction of staff when confronted with a possible email identity theft situation.

Test 4 - An apparently legitimate email was send to users to convince them to run an executable file. The users were given bait in the form of a message that invited them to run an executable file that will improve their computers' performance. This was an unfamiliar named file and the aim was to determine if users reacted responsibly by not executing strange files.

2.2 Methodology used

The process followed to conduct the exercise is described in [6] and is briefly repeated here. The complete process, including all four tests, was handled in three phases – two test phases and the final test. As an initial test, the email messages were sent to the authors to test the technical working of the program and to verify whether the statistics were recorded correctly. The second phase was a small pilot run where messages were sent to a small number of randomly selected staff members – the aim was to determine if everything operates correctly when sending the messages outside of the technical test environment and also to try and determine what reactions or enquiries could be received.

For the final test it was decided to send the message to a sample of staff and to assist with the sampling process the electronic campus address book, which is publicly available to all staff, was used as the population. There were approximately 2400 use-able records in the address book and the sample size, n, for each one of the four tests, was determined as $n = e^{-2}$, where e is the accuracy of the estimated proportion with a 95% confidence [7]. For the purpose of this study, e was chosen to be 0,05 which re-sulted in a sample size of 400 for each of the four tests. Once the sample size was de-termined, it was decided to select staff by making use of the systematic sampling method [8]. Sampling begins by randomly selecting the first observation. Thereafter subsequent observations are selected at a uniform interval relative to the first observa-tion. The ratio N/n, where N is the population size and n the sample size, provides the interval length – for this study, N was approximately 2400 and $n = 400$ which means that every 6th element (staff member) was chosen to receive the email message for each of the tests.

The email messages were sent to the 1600 (400 per test) randomly selected staff members and provision was made to receive phone calls and direct email replies from staff. After seven days the exercise was declared closed and the recorded data was analysed. A discussion of results follows in the next section.

3   Results

The main result of interest was to determine how many employees in each of the four tests were trapped. The term "trapped" is used for those cases where the users' reac-tion was not in line with expected behaviour, e.g. to give a password away as opposed to not give it away.

Table 1 shows the main outcome of how many employees were trapped in each of the four tests. For example, in test 1, the message on personal finances, 295 (73.8%) from the sample of 400 users opened the mail message; of these, 148 (50.2%) were not trapped (did not follow the HTML link) and 147 (49.8%) were trapped by follow-ing the link. Figure 1 is a graphical representation of the figures.

Table 1. Behaviour data

Tests	Emails opened	Opened not trapped	Opened and trapped
Test 1	295	148 (50.2%)	147 (49.8%)
Test 2	213	160 (75.1%)	53 (24.9%)
Test 3	320	149 (46.6%)	171 (53.4%)
Test 4	265	148 (55.8%)	117 (44.2%)

It is interesting to note that tests 1 and 3 (personal finances and personal informa-tion), were more readily opened. There were also a fair number of employees who opened the message of test 4 (computer performance) while less users opened the message from test 2 (virus checker). The fact that only 53 of the 213 users were trapped with the virus checker message may indicate that there is a certain degree of awareness related to virus threats. At the same time it is disappointing that 50% of users were trapped in test 1 and more than half was willing to give their passwords away in test 3. These figures should be considered high given the environment and the above average level of computer literacy of staff.

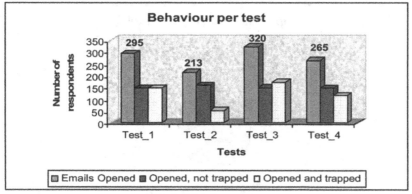

Fig. 1. Behaviour per test

Figure 2 presents the sample distribution of staff for all four tests over the 8 different divisions, e.g. Natural Sciences, Economic and Management Sciences etc., as well as a ninth one which represents the non-academic component.

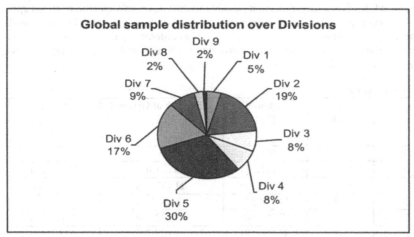

Fig. 2. Sample distribution over divisions

The distribution of employees, who were trapped in all four tests, is shown in figure 3. Although it is strongly related to the sample distribution in figure 2, it does provide certain insight into possible higher risk groups. For example, division 5 had 30% of the employees that were sampled (fig 2) and 35% of the employees that were trapped (fig 3). Clearly division 5 is a higher risk group than, for example, division 6 where the proportions were 17% and 14% respectively.

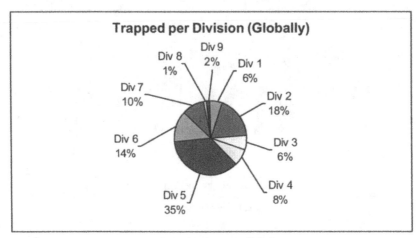

Fig. 3. Behaviour per division

The statistics so far are on a fairly high level. However, the design of the experiment and the data obtained made it possible to drill down into specific tests and specific divisions to such a level where the information becomes very significant and meaningful to management. The constraints of a conference paper prohibit a detailed presentation and explanation of such drill down activities and the following short example should suffice.

Table 2. Drill down data for test 2

Test 2	Sample size	Opened (%)	Delete - Not Opened (%)	Trapped (%)
Div 1	19	13 (68.42)	5 (26.32)	4 (30.77)
Div 2	76	39 (51.32)	16 (21.05)	11 (28.21)
Div 3	34	12 (35.29)	11 (32.35)	5 (41.67)
Div 4	29	14 (48.28)	7 (24.14)	3 (21.43)
Div 5	120	69 (57.50)	27 (22.50)	19 (27.54)
Div 6	69	39 (56.52)	19 (27.54)	6 (15.38)
Div 7	37	20 (54.0)	9 (24.32)	5 (25.00)
Div 8	9	3 (33.33)	5 (55.56)	0 (0.00)
Div 9	7	4 (57.14)	1 (14.29)	0 (0.00)
Total	**400**	**213 (53.25)**	**100 (25.00)**	**53 (24.88)**

Detailed figures per division for specific tests can be constructed. In table 2 such figures for test 2 are presented.

In the "Sample size" column, the number of employees per division, selected in the sample is shown. This is followed by the number and percentage of employees per division that opened the message. The "Delete (Not opened)" column indicates the number and percentage of people who deleted the email message, during the 7 days of the experiment, without opening it. It should be noted that the numbers in this column and the numbers in the "opened" column do not necessarily add up to the sample size. This is due to the fact that there were certain cases where overlapping of reactions were possible e.g. staff who was on leave during the exercise and who did not open or delete the messages. The last column indicates those that were trapped per division. From this table it is easy to see, for test 2, that an awareness campaign should not be a high priority in divisions 8 and 9 but rather be focused on divisions 3, 1, 2, and 5. Figure 4 shows the detailed figures from table 2 in graph form.

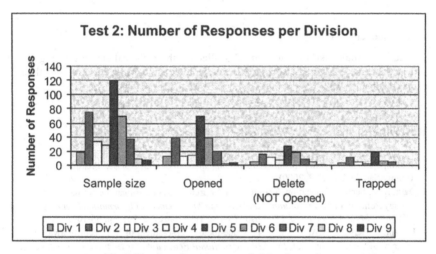

Fig. 4. Number of responses per division for test 2

The reported figures and data presentations in this paper are by no means a comprehensive report on the email awareness assessment and more detailed analyses and interpretations are possible. An important lesson from this assessment, however, was the confirmation that a significant number of users are irresponsible in certain situations. The temptations should be identified and acted upon and the results from the reported exercise should be helpful to indicate whereto and on what level awareness campaigns can be considered. The next section concludes the paper.

4   Conclusion

This paper has described a practical assessment of employees' awareness pertaining to responsible email usage. The experiment was performed as part of a bigger ICT security awareness project to obtain objective system data on users' behaviour. The results have shown that users generally acted irresponsibly in some of the tests, e.g. most users were trapped by emails regarding their personal finances and personal information. More than 50% of employees were willing to disclose their passwords. On the positive side employees appear to be more aware of virus threats.

The data obtained in these tests can be used for educational and training purposes in security awareness programmes. Not only can divisions be identified where guidance is needed but the specific types of threats that users are exposed to can also be identified. These results are made available to IT management and they are in a position now to address specific problem areas.

Future work will include the incorporation of the results obtained here with other system generated data. These tests can also be extended to other campuses or companies for comparative research purposes.

Acknowledgements

The authors would like to thank Mr. C Muller for the technical support during the four email tests. We would also like to thank the three anonymous reviewers for their useful feedback.

References

1. Pipkin, D.L.: *Information Security. Protecting the Global Enterprise.* Prentice-Hall Inc., (Upper Saddle River, NJ, 2000)
2. Dark, M.J.: Security Education, Training and Awareness from a Human Performance Technology Point of View, *In: Readings and Cases in Management of Information Security, Whitman, M.E., Mattord, H.J.* (Thomson Course Technology, 2006), pp. 86-104.
3. Drevin, L., Kruger, H.A. & Steyn, T.: Value-focused assessment of ICT security awareness in an academic environment, *In: IFIP International Federation for Information Processing, Volume 201, Security and Privacy in Dynamic Environments, eds. Fischer-Hubner, S., Ranneberg, K., Yngstrom, L., Lindskog, S.* (Boston: Springer, 2006), pp. 448-453.
4. Dodge, R.C. & Ferguson, A.J.: Using Phishing for User Email Security Awareness, *In: IFIP International Federation for Information Processing, Volume 201, Security and Privacy in Dynamic Environments, eds. Fischer-Hubner, S., Ranneberg, K., Yngstrom, L., Lindskog, S.* (Boston: Springer, 2006), pp. 454-459.
5. Kruger, H.A., Drevin, L. & Steyn, T.: A framework for evaluating ICT security awareness, *In: Proceedings of the 2006 ISSA Conference, Johannesburg, South Africa,* 5-7 July 2006 (on CD, 2006).
6. Steyn, T., Kruger, H.A. & Drevin, L.: Identity theft – Empirical evidence from a Phishing exercise, *In: Proceedings of the 2007 IFIP Conference, Sandton, South Africa,14-*16 May 2007 (Accepted, to be published, 2007).
7. Steyn, A.G.W., Smit, C.F., Du Toit, S.H.C. & Strasheim, C.: *Moderne Statistiek vir die Praktyk.* Sesde uitgawe. (JL van Schaik. Pretoria, 1998).
8. Wegner, T.: *Applied Business Statistics.* (Juta & Co, Ltd. Kenwyn, 1993).

SecSDM: A Model for Integrating Security into the Software Development Life Cycle

Lynn Futcher, Rossouw von Solms

Centre for Information Security Studies,
Nelson Mandela Metropolitan University,
Port Elizabeth, South Africa
{Lynn.Futcher, Rossouw.VonSolms}@nmmu.ac.za

Abstract. Most traditional software development methodologies do not explicitly include a standardised method for incorporating information security into their life cycles. It is argued that security considerations should provide input into every phase of the Software Development Life Cycle (SDLC), from requirements gathering to design, implementation, testing and deployment. Therefore, to build more secure software applications, an improved software development process is required. The Secure Software Development Model (SecSDM), as described in this paper, is based on many of the recommendations provided by relevant international standards and best practices, for example, the ISO 7498-2 (1989) standard which addresses the underlying security services and mechanisms that form an integral part of the model.

Keywords: Risk analysis, secure software development, security mechanisms, security services.

1   Introduction

It is within highly integrated technology environments that information security is becoming a focal point for designing, developing and deploying software applications. Ensuring a high level of trust in the security and quality of these applications is crucial to their ultimate success. Therefore, information security has become a core requirement for software applications, driven by the need to protect critical assets and the need to build and preserve widespread trust in computing.

A Microsoft study demonstrated that 64% of software developers are not confident in their ability to write secure applications [1]. This is despite the fact that the .Net framework and Visual Studio.Net provide them with the necessary tools and information to write secure applications. Software developers often rely on their intuition in developing secure software and do so without much systematic help or guidance. These professionals need be educated to put security at both the heart of software design and at the foundation of its development process [2]. This implies that software developers need to use improved processes that consistently produce secure software. Currently, no software development processes or practices exist that consistently produce secure software [3]. It is therefore recommended that software producers adopt

Please use the following format when citing this chapter:

Futcher, L., von Solms, R., 2007, in IFIP International Federation for Information Processing, Volume 237, Fifth World Conference on Information Security Education, eds. Futcher, L., Dodge, R., (Boston: Springer), pp. 41–48.

practices that can measurably reduce software specification, design and implementation defects and, therefore, minimise any potential risk.

This paper describes a model for integrating security into the SDLC. It proposes a more stringent software development methodology that both detects and removes vulnerabilities early in the life cycle, thereby minimising the number of security vulnerabilities in the live system. The SecSDM aims to draw attention to the importance of security in the SDLC. It is designed as an extension, not a replacement, to pre-existing software development methodologies.

2   The Software Development Life Cycle

The development of software has always been regarded as a difficult task. For this reason, many different methodologies have been proposed by various researchers to guide the software development process as a whole. Software development typically follows a life cycle which determines the phases along which the software product moves. The traditional SDLC is a methodology for the design and implementation of an information system in an organisation. There are many representations of the SDLC, all showing a logical flow of activity from the identification of a need to the final software product. Each methodology has its own strengths and weaknesses and is therefore well-suited for certain types of applications. Although more complex systems require more iterative development models, the five phases comprising the traditional linear SDLC model are inherent in most software development methodologies and therefore form the basis for the SecSDM.

If security considerations were woven into the SDLC, many of the security vulnerabilities that manifest themselves in live systems today would never appear [4]. Therefore, it is argued that a more stringent software development process that incorporates security is required. Such a process should minimise the number of security vulnerabilities present in the SDLC and detect and remove these vulnerabilities as early in the life cycle as possible [5]. New ways of addressing and resolving security issues, early within the SDLC, must be introduced in the software development arena [6].

Although many researchers advocate that security needs to be integrated into the SDLC, few are able to describe a process to achieve this goal. It is argued that the evident separation between information security and software development has resulted in the production of vulnerable software applications. Therefore, it is necessary to develop an improved software development process to build more secure software. Security concerns must provide input into every phase of the SDLC.

3   The Secure Software Development Model

Various international standards and best practices were consulted when developing this model. These include ISO/IEC 17799 [7], the international code of practice for information security management, the guidelines of the detailed risk analysis approach as determined by ISO/IEC TR 13335-3 [8], the NIST SP 800-14 [9] which outlines generally accepted principles and practices for securing information technology systems, and ISO 7498-2 [11] which provides the basis of information security in software systems through five basic security services, supported by eight security mechanisms.

An important consideration in developing this model was to define a useable process that will lessen the burden for software developers who are not specialists in information security. This section describes the SecSDM as a simple, ten-step process for integrating security concerns into each phase of the SDLC as follows:

- *Investigation Phase*: determines the security requirements of the software application by executing a simple risk analysis exercise;
  - STEP 1: Information asset identification and valuation;
  - STEP 2: Threat identification and assessment;
  - STEP 3: Risk (asset/threat) identification;
  - STEP 4: Determine the level of vulnerability;
  - STEP 5: Risk assessment;
  - STEP 6: Risk prioritisation.
- *Analysis Phase*: determines the security services to be used to satisfy the security requirements;
  - STEP 7: Identify the relevant security services and level of protection required to mitigate each risk.
- *Design Phase*: determines how the security services will be implemented;
  - STEP 8: Map security services to security mechanisms;
  - STEP 9: Consolidate security services and mechanisms.
- *Implementation Phase*: identifies and implements appropriate software security tools and components;
  - STEP 10: Map security mechanisms to software security components.
- *Maintenance Phase*: the maintenance of software is made easier and more manageable through the structured approach provided by the SecSDM. Users and operations staff need to be educated in using the software application in a secure manner.

3.1   The investigation phase

Early determination of security requirements is necessary to develop software applications which can be trusted by all stakeholders. ISO/IEC TR 13335-3 [8] suggests that information security requirements are stated in terms of confidentiality, integrity, availability, accountability, authenticity and reliability of information. Therefore, it is necessary to perform some form of a risk analysis to determine the security requirements of a particular system.

The proposed risk analysis approach carried out during the investigation phase takes the form of a step-by-step process. Its purpose is to identify the information assets, their associated threats and vulnerabilities, and rank them according to those assets that need the most protection. Different industries and different systems have varying information protection requirements. For example, healthcare organisations stress the confidentiality of patient records, whereas banking is more concerned about the integrity of monetary transactions. The software development team needs to understand and capture what the adequate protection of information is, in their specific context [11].

STEP 1: Information asset identification and valuation

The listing of assets based on checklists and judgment, yields an adequate identification of the important assets associated with the software application being developed [12]. These information assets can include, for example, personal information, employee salary information, customer contact information or financial information.

The next step in the process is to assign values to each of the key information assets identified. This is necessary to determine the impact value and sensitivity of the information in use, stored, processed or accessed. The SecSDM uses a 5-point Lickert scale and requires that an asset impact value between 0 and 4 (where 0=negligible and 4=critical) be assigned to each of the key information assets identified. These values represent the business importance of the assets and will typically be obtained by interviewing the information owners and its key users. The next step requires the identification of the various threats that may cause harm to these assets.

STEP 2: Threat identification and assessment

It is necessary to perform the identification and assessment of threats during the investigation phase of the SDLC. This information is required to identify risks and to guide subsequent design, coding and testing decisions.

A checklist of the most common threats is provided by the SecSDM, based on those referred to in ISO/IEC TR 13335-3 [8]. Such a checklist of the most likely threats is helpful in performing a threat assessment, although software developers must be aware that threats are continually changing. Furthermore, it is necessary, as part of the threat assessment process, to determine the potential impact that each of the common threats may have on the assets associated with the software application. This may be performed, according to the SecSDM, by assigning each of the threats identified to one of the likelihood levels (low, medium or high).

STEP 3: Risk (asset/threat) identification

Risk identification requires that the most critical asset/threat relationships are identified to ascertain which risks are most likely to impact the proposed system [13]. This is done by simply considering the key information assets, as identified in Step 1, and the most likely threats identified in Step 2. Those assets with high or critical asset impact values (i.e., 3 or 4) and those threats recognised to have a potentially high impact will contribute significantly to the criticality of the risk. The following step in the process requires that the level of vulnerability for each critical risk be determined.

STEP 4: Determine the level of vulnerability

In practice, security is not compromised by breaking the dedicated security mechanisms, but by exploiting the weaknesses or vulnerabilities in the way they are used [2]. Therefore, as part of the risk analysis process, it is important to be able to determine the level of vulnerability for each risk. It is necessary to consider the likelihood that the risk may materialise, taking the current situation and controls into account, to determine the level of weakness or vulnerability for each risk. The three main levels of vulnerability provided by this model are low, medium and high. The following step in the risk analysis process requires that a risk assessment be carried out to determine the extent of each risk.

STEP 5: Risk assessment

The extent of risk is determined, according to the SecSDM, by taking into account the asset impact value, level of vulnerability and potential likelihood of each threat identified. These are matched in a lookup table to establish the specific measure of risk on a scale of 1 to 8. The specific risk values established are determined according to those recommended by ISO/IEC TR 13335-3 [8].

STEP 6: Risk prioritization

The prioritisation of risks during the investigation phase serves as a guideline for the analysis, design and implementation phases of the SDLC. This is achieved by simply listing each risk, identified in Step 3, and its corresponding risk value as established in Step 5.

3.2   The analysis phase

The risk extent of a particular software application determines the scope of the security services employed. Therefore, it is meaningful for the analysis phase to focus on the security risks as identified during the investigation phase. During the analysis phase, security services are selected according to their ability to mitigate the security risks identified. It is important, however, that this is carried out independently of any implementation details. The output of this phase is a refined set of security requirements.

The ISO 7498-2 standard provides the basis for information security in software applications through five basic security services, namely: identification and authentication, authorisation/access control, confidentiality, integrity and non-repudiation/non-denial. These five security services provide the basis for ensuring the security of any software application [10].

STEP 7: Identify the relevant security services and level of protection required to minimise each risk

Software developers are required to map each of the most critical risks, as identified during the investigation phase, to the envisaged security services. For each risk, multiple security services may be identified. However, not all security services are required to address each individual risk, and neither are all security services applicable to all risks. This step results in the appropriate level of protection being selected to reduce the risks to an acceptable level. The next section describes the process of selecting the appropriate security mechanisms through which the security services, identified in Step 7, should be implemented.

3.3   The design phase

It is during the design phase of the SecSDM that the security services need to be translated into security mechanisms. The five security services referred to by ITU-T X.800 and the ISO 7498-2 standard are supported by eight security mechanisms, namely: encipherment, digital signatures, access control, data integrity, authentication exchange, traffic padding, routing control and notarisation [10]. These security mechanisms, however, cannot be "blindly" inserted into a software application in the hope of providing the required level of security. The overall system development process needs to take the various security concerns and risks into consideration to ensure the appropriate use of the required security mechanisms.

STEP 8: Map security services to security mechanisms

The SecSDM provides guidelines to assist software developers in selecting the most appropriate security mechanisms to support the security services identified during the analysis phase. For example, if confidentiality is a required security service, then encryption can be used as the security mechanism. The mapping of security services to the appropriate security mechanisms is required for all risks identified during the investigation phase.

STEP 9: Consolidate security services and mechanisms.

For ease of implementation, the SecSDM requires the consolidation of the results of Steps 7 and 8. Software developers are required to map the various security mechanisms to the appropriate security services for each risk, as identified during the investigation phase.

3.4   The implementation phase

During the previous phases, according to the SecSDM, the risk sensitivity of the system has been determined and the most appropriate security services and mechanisms to be employed have been identified. These mechanisms need to be implemented. The implementation of security mechanisms depends on the programming language used, the coding standards and best practices adhered to, and the personal programming style of the programmer. It is important to ensure that developers are knowledgeable about security risks and skilled in secure coding standards [4]. The programmer must ensure that all security-relevant code is understandable, auditable, maintainable and testable [14].

An important part of the implementation phase is testing. Testing is often seen as a way of 'testing in' security which is unacceptable. The role of security testing is to verify that the system design and code can withstand attack. Testing ensures that countermeasures are correctly implemented and that code is developed following coding standards and best practices. Security testing should follow a security test plan. This test plan should include unit testing, integration testing, quality assurance testing and penetration testing [4]. The testing of the software to validate that it meets the security requirements as determined during the investigation phase is essential to produce secure software. This testing should include serious attempts to attack and break its security and scan for common vulnerabilities [3].

STEP 10: Map security mechanisms to software security components.
The security mechanisms identified may be implemented through appropriate software security tools and components, for example, those inherent in the .Net framework. The .Net framework provides developers with the necessary tools and information to write secure applications [1]. The SecSDM does not currently recommend the use of specific software security components to implement the various security mechanisms. However, it does describe the process of mapping the security mechanisms summarised in Step 9 to various software security components as recommended by the software developer. An implementation priority list is needed which indicates the priority of the security mechanisms to be implemented to ensure that the correct security features are employed [15]. Therefore, software developers are encouraged to indicate the specific software security components through which the various security mechanisms will be implemented.

3.5   The maintenance phase

The maintenance phase is often viewed as another iteration of the entire life cycle [16]. During this phase, it is important to find ways to evaluate the security of the system to ensure that the system is as secure as intended. The SecSDM ensures that all relevant security-related information is well documented. This helps improve the auditability of the software application in question, because security-related decisions are traceable to the appropriate phase as proposed by this secure software development approach. The integration of information security into the SDLC as described in this section, and the tight integration between the various phases will help ensure that the final product meets the information security requirements, identified during the initial phases.

4   Conclusion

By applying the SecSDM, security is tightly interwoven in the software development process. Software developers are encouraged to consider security from the earliest phases of the SDLC, and to build critical security milestones and events into their development timelines. The concepts from each phase of the SecSDM should be integrated into the corresponding phases of the existing SDLC to ensure that security is appropriately considered and built into the software application. This type of inclusion should result in a robust end product that is more secure, easier to maintain and less costly to own.

The SecSDM, as described in this paper, has been implemented with an associated methodology at a tertiary institution. Initial experiments have shown encouraging results. A further positive aspect is that the associated documentation ensures that the entire security analysis and implementation process is auditable.

References

1. Taft, D. K. (2004, Dec). Microsoft aids secure coding. eWeek.
2. Jurjens, J. (2002, May). Using UMLSec and goal trees for secure systems development. Communications of the ACM, 48 (5), pp.1026-1030.
3. Task Force Report. (2004, April). Improving security across the software development life cycle (Technical Report). National Cyber Security Summit.
4. Jones, R. L.& Rastogi, A. (2004, Nov). Secure coding - building security into the software development life cycle. Application Program Security, pp.29-38.
5. Lipner, S.& Howard, M. (2005). The trustworthy computing security development lifecycle. 27. (cited on 15th April 2005)
6. Tryfonas, T.& Kiountouzis, E. (2002). Information systems security and the information systems development project. In Proceedings of IFIP.
7. ISO. (2005). ISO/IEC 17799 : Information Technology - Code of Practice for Information Security Management.
8. ISO. (1998). ISO/IEC TR 13335-3 : Information Technology – Guidelines for the Management of IT Security. Part 3 : Techniques for the management of IT security.
9. NIST (1996, Sept). Generally accepted principles and practices for securing information technology systems. NIST Special Publication 800-14. (http://csrc.nist.gov/publications)
10. ISO. (1989). ISO 7498-2: Information Processing Systems - Open System Interconnection - Basic Reference Model - Part 2: Security Architecture.
11. Tipton, H. F.& Krause, M. (2006). Information security management handbook (Fifth ed., Vol. 3). New York : United States of America: Auerbach Publications.
12. Landoll, D. J. (2006). The security risk assessment handbook : A complete guide for performing security risk assessments. New York : United States of America: Auerbach Publications.
13. Whitman, M.& Mattord, M. (2003). Principles of information security. Thomson Course Technology.
14. Tompkins, F. G.& Rice, R. (1985). Integrating security activities into the software development life cycle and the quality assurance process. In Proceedings of IFIP pp.65-105.
15. Siponen, M., Baskerville, R.& Kuivalainen, T. (2005). Integrating security into agile development methods. In Proceedings of the 38th Hawaii international conference on system sciences.
16. Gregory, P. H. (2003). Security in the software development life cycle (Technical Report). The Hart Gregory Group Inc.

A CBK for Information Security and Critical Infrastructure Protection

Marianthi Theoharidou, Eleftheria Stougiannou, Dimitris Gritzalis

Information Security and Critical Infrastructure Protection Research Group,
Dept. of Informatics, Athens University of Economics and Business,
76 Patission Ave., Athens, GR-10434, Greece
{mtheohar, estoug, dgrit}@aueb.gr

Abstract. Academic institutions educate future Information Security and Critical Infrastructure Protection (ISCIP) professionals, offering expedient and broad knowledge of the field. As industry often demands higher productivity and stronger specialization, several organizations (academic, governmental, industrial) considered the use of a Common Body of Knowledge (CBK), to serve as a tool that appropriately groups together the essential knowledge of this field. In this paper, we review the content of current ISCIP curricula, we define the necessary skills of an ISCIP Professional - as indicated and suggested by the industry - and form a multidisciplinary CBK of the ISCIP field.

Keywords: Common Body of Knowledge (CBK), Academic Curriculum, Academic Programme, Critical Infrastructure Protection.

1 Introduction

The demand for Information Security and Critical Infrastructure Protection (ISCIP) professionals is usually addressed by academia, in an expedient and broad way [10]. From its side, industry expects high productivity and strong specialization [4]; thus, it expects from academic institutions to focus mostly on "applied security", and give comparatively less emphasis to the "principles" [3]. The resulting "gap" is usually bridged by training courses and seminars [12], as well as industry-initiated and supported certifications on various security-related topics [8, 9].

The need for skilful ISCIP professionals led several organizations (academic, governmental, industrial) to consider the development of a Common Body of Knowledge (CBK) for the security domain. A CBK is "a collection of information and a framework that provides a basis for understanding terms and concepts in a particular knowledge area. It also provides a set of basic information that people who work in that knowledge area are expected to know"[1]. According to the International Information Systems Security Certifications Consortium (ISC)², a CBK is defined as "a taxonomy - a collection of topics relevant to information security professionals around the world" (www.isc2.org). In this paper, we consider a CBK as a conceptual means that define the knowledge, which is considered essential for the cognitive background and the required skills of a professional.

Please use the following format when citing this chapter:

Theoharidou, M., Stougiannou, E., Gritzalis, D., 2007, in IFIP International Federation for Information Processing, Volume 237, Fifth World Conference on Information Security Education, eds. Futcher, L., Dodge, R., (Boston: Springer), pp. 49-56.

Several of the existing CBK efforts were initiated by the industry, mostly for certification processes of security professionals (e.g., CISSP, GIAC, CISA, etc.). One may refer to the (ISC)² CBK, which is used for certifying CISSP Professionals and receives wide recognition. It focuses on establishing a common framework of information security terms and principles, which would allow information security professionals to discuss, debate, and resolve relevant issues. It includes ten "domains" [6] and it reflects mostly the industry needs. However, its adaptation for security curricula suffers by the risk of adopting solely the practitioner's view of security.

Typical academic examples include a CBK for "Information Assurance" [3], a CBK for "Information Security in Network Technologies" [7], and a CBK for Information Security professionals [10]. These few in number efforts do not aim at providing a security CBK, but they focus on a sub-domain and serve as a guide to create a course or a curriculum [3, 7]. The CBK for "Information Security in Network Technologies" [7] provides only a schematic representation of the field, without any details about how the CBK was developed. The Information Security CBK [10] focuses on minimizing the perceived "gap" between the academia and the industry, but it is quite generic, as its main goal is to prove the concept and not give an extensive CBK. It divides the Information Security field in technical and non technical topics.

A recent governmental initiative resulted in a CBK for "Secure Software Assurance" for the U.S. Dept. of Homeland Security [1, 8]. It provides a basis for the "secure software engineering" discipline and educators can use this guide to identify both, appropriate curricular content, as well as references that detail it. The guide is designed to cover the need of the US government to procure secure software.

We consider that ISCIP is a multidisciplinary endeavor [5, 13]. For its better understanding, analysis and practice, a professional should use knowledge from fields such as management, business administration, law, ethics, sociology, political science, criminology, didactic, etc. However, none of these CBK covers ISCIP in such a way. They seem to focus on specific sub-domains of ISCIP (e.g. CBK suggested by [3, 7]), thus offering limited understanding and a narrow perception of the ISCIP as a whole.

2 Methodology for CBK Development

We aim at identifying, defining and conceptually presenting a multidisciplinary CBK for ISCIP, which may serve as a tool for developing an ISCIP curricula. We will take into account the expectations of the industry, in an effort to bridge the "gap". In order to do so, we followed a three-step approach.

Step 1: We identified the industry and academic views on this issue, by performing:

(1a). A survey on curricula and courses (Section 3). As ISCIP is dealt within different curricula, we chose and focus on those university programmes, which are related to the "information scene". As a result, we selected (undergraduate and postgraduate) programmes on computer science, business administration, information systems management, sociology, and law, that either offer an academic degree on ISCIP, or offer courses on, or related to, ISCIP.

(1b). A survey on the industry demand for ISCIP professionals, in order to identify the excepted skills of an ISCIP professional. We consulted the Career Space Consortium (www.career-space.com), a coalition which includes eleven major ICT companies and the European I&CT Industry Association. It defines Generic Skills Profiles for ICT professionals. From the existing profiles we selected those related to ISCIP. With these into account, we reviewed the current demand, regarding the required knowledge and skills of a professional, and enriched the skill set.

Step 2: After the surveys were completed, we defined: (a) the structure and (b) the content of an ISCIP CBK. We first selected the disciplines that were identified to be closely related to ISCIP. Then, we identified the prerequisite knowledge by other disciplines, which an ISCIP professional must acquire.

Step 3: We developed a hierarchy of concepts and elements needed in order to develop the CBK. A top-down approach was adopted and the hierarchy was filled up with elements, according to the university curricula we had examined in the relevant survey. After the hierarchy was complete, it was checked against the skills/knowledge set, as defined by our survey. Then, we combined the elements and grouped them under a common "root", so as to create a classification of the topics. The result was a CBK with ten domains, where each domain is analyzed in a more detailed level.

3 ISCIP Programmes and Courses: A Survey

The first step was to identify the structure and the content of the current ISCIP programmes and courses. In total, we studied 135 academic institutions, which offer curricula on: Computer Science, Information Systems, Management, Engineering, Business Administration, or Law. We selected them based on a) their quality, b) their faculty and c) their geographical position. Our survey was based on an online search through university websites, as well as a study of their syllabi. It indicated that 15 institutions, at the undergraduate level, and 45, at the postgraduate level, offer degrees of some kind on ISCIP. Most of them are run under the umbrella of either a Computer Science or a Computer Engineering Department. Several offer, usually optional, ISCIP courses, without offering a degree on ISCIP. From those that offer ISCIP degrees, only few syllabi include courses from other disciplines. Examples include skills like written/oral communication, public speaking, ethics, law, and management. Table 1 refers to the content of ISCIP courses, presented in 7 categories.

Table 1. ISCIP courses content.

Category	Usual content of ISCIP Courses
Access Control and Privacy	Identification, Authentication, Access Control, Authorization, Anonymity, Privacy
Risk and Attacks	Attacks, Vulnerabilities, Risks, Intrusion Detection, Malicious Software, Tests and Audits, Safeguards, Intrusion Handling
Cryptography	Applied Cryptography, Digital Signatures/Certificates, Key Management, PKI
Networks	Security Theory, Protocols and Algorithms, Firewalls
Security Design	Design of Computer Systems Security
Business	Business Continuity Plan
Other	Ethical and Legal Issues

4 Skills of an ISCIP Professional: a review

In order to develop a CBK, one has to determine the skills that are needed when dealing with ISCIP problems. We first chose the ICT professional areas[1], as defined by the Career Space Consortium, which refer to specific security knowledge. In order to do so, we studied the content of the security courses that we identified in the previous section. Then, we listed the skills required by the chosen ICT categories professionals. Table 2 includes the skill set of an ISCIP Professional. The order of appearance is random and all the skills are considered equally important.

Table 2. Technical and Behavioural skills of an ISCIP professional.

Category	Skills
ICT	Networks, Technology and Computer Engineering, Systems Design and Architecture, Programming, Software Development, Mathematics, Statistics, Project Management, Business Strategy and Requirements Analysis, Testing, Basic Security Skills, Technical Documentation, System Management, Quality Assurance, Evaluation and Configuration Methodologies.
Security	Information Security and Human Computer Interaction, Computer Forensics, Database Security and Data Mining, Operation Systems Security, Security Architecture, Malicious Software, Internet and Cyber-security, Incident Handling, Hacking, Cryptography, Biometric Techniques, Smart Cards, Auditing, Data and Infrastructure Protection, Risk Management.
Behavioural	Leadership, Ethics, Analytical & Conceptual Thinking, Perspicacity, Creative Thought, Knowing one's limits, Professional Attitude, Communication, Technical Orientation & Interest, Customer Orientation, Strategy & Planning, Writing & Presentation skills, Efficiency & Quality, Applying Knowledge.

5 CBK Development

This CBK aims at reconciling industry and academia, by taking into account the results of the surveys we have conducted, and, at the same time, reflects the multidisciplinary nature of ISCIP [5, 11, 13]. Practically, we cover thirteen "Dimensions of Information Security", namely Governance/Organizational, Ethical, Awareness, Policy, Certification, Measurement/Metrics, Best Practice, Legal, Technical, Strategic/Corporate Governance, Insurance, Audit, and Personnel/Human [11]. We developed the ISCIP CBK in a top-down approach. We identified several fundamental disciplines, and then the CBK was further analyzed in more specific concepts. First, we identified seven ISCIP related disciplines: Computer Science, Computer Engineering, Law, Sociology/Criminology, Ethics/Psychology, Business and Information Systems Management, and Didactic. Then, we identified and described the prerequisite knowledge that

---

[1] Integration and Test Engineering, Systems Specialist, Data Communication Engineering, DSP-Application Design, Technical Support, Communication Network Design, Software and Application Development, Software Architecture and Design, Research and Technology Development, ICT Management, IT Business Consultancy, ICT Project Management.

must be incorporated by other disciplines. Based on the seven CBK disciplines, we categorized the security courses identified in the first survey, as well as the skills i-dentified in the second survey. An hierarchy was then formed. We added as elements all the topics found, following a top-down approach. The final step was to combine the related elements of the different disciplines and to group these elements under a common "root". Then, we grouped the knowledge in ten domains, presented in Table 3.

Table 3. ISCIP CBK domains.

Domain
1. Security Architecture and Models
2. Access Control Systems and Methodology
3. Cryptography
4. Networks and Telecommunications Security
5. Operating Systems Security
6. Program and Application Security
7. Database Security
8. Business and Management of Information Systems Security
9. Physical Security and Critical Infrastructure Protection
10. Social, Ethical and Legal Aspects of Security

Each general domain is then analyzed into sub-domains. A selection of seven domains is schematically presented in the Appendix (Fig. 1-7)[2]. Each element of them can be further analyzed in more detailed sub-elements. Here, we present the elements up to their second level of analysis. One should note that some elements are included in more than one domain and that, in each domain, the disciplines each topic mainly de-rives from are graphically presented.

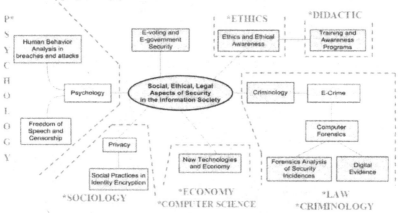

Fig. 1. Social, Ethical, and Legal Aspects of Security (Domain 10)

---

[2] An earlier version of this paper appears in the IEEE Security & Privacy, Vol. 4, No. 2, pp. 64-67, March/April 2007.

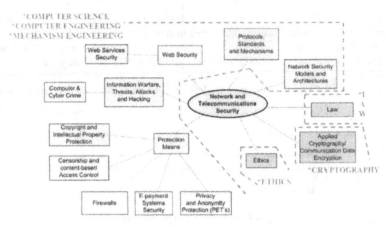

Fig. 2. Network and Telecommunications Security (Domain 4)

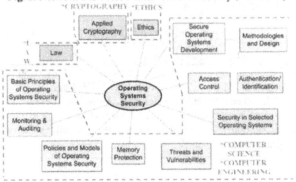

Fig. 3. Operating Systems Security (Domain 5)

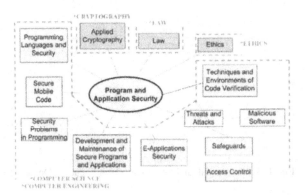

Fig. 4. Program and Application Security (Domain 6)

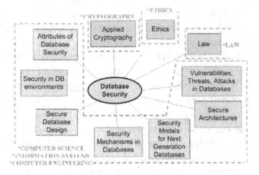

Fig. 5. Database Security (Domain 7)

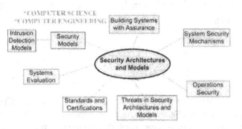

Fig. 6. Security Architecture and Models (Domain 1)

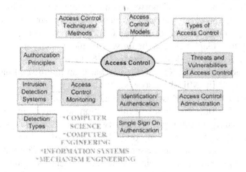

Fig. 7. Access Control Systems and Methodology (Domain 2)

6 Conclusions

We reviewed the content of current ISCIP curricula and courses, formed a skill set of the ISCIP Professional and, based on these, we formed a broad ISCIP CBK that encompasses seven disciplines. We designed the CBK to serve as a tool when designing a curricula or course in ISCIP. It is presented in two levels of analysis and categorizes the knowledge of the field. Nevertheless, this CBK has not been applied thoroughly, so evaluation results are not yet available. We will improve and evaluate it, when we observe and document its use in the design of academic courses or curricula, which is one of our future goals. One idea is to restructure a course in ISCIP, based on this CBK, either an introductory course or a more specific one based on one or two domains. Furthermore, an ISCIP CBK needs to be constantly refined in order to fit into the emerging context and content of the field, so this is an ongoing process. The ten domains most likely will remain the same for some time, however, we expect their elements to transform regularly. Its application may also introduce refinements, additions or different groupings. We have to point out that this CBK was initially formed to assist on curricula design. Therefore, it is intended to be abstract and generic, as it attempts to group and categorize all the ISCIP knowledge, and not a specific ISCIP topic of interest (e.g. Information Assurance). This is the reason why it does not include the content and the teaching material of the knowledge elements and only their structure. We believe that this CBK can help the teacher structure the contents of his course or curricula and then he can enrich its course material from commonly accepted sources.

References

1. Bishop M., Engle S.: The Software Assurance CBK and University Curricula. 10th Colloquium for Information Systems Security Education. University of Maryland, USA (2006). Available online at: http://nob.cs.ucdavis.edu/bishop/talks/2006-cisse-1/swacbk.pdf.
2. Cabay M.: Information security education resources for professional development, ver. 11 (2004). Available online at: www2.norwich.edu/mkabay/overviews/infosec_ed.pdf.
3. Crowley E.: Information system security curricula development. In: Brewer J., Mendonca J. (Eds.): Proc. of the 4th Conf. on ITechnology Curriculum. ACM Press, USA (2003).
4. Egan L.: Closing the "Gap" between the university and industry in computer science. ACM SIGCSE Bulletin, Vol. 8, No. 4. ACM Press (1976) 19-25.
5. Gritzalis D., Theocharidou M., Kalimeri E.: Towards an interdisciplinary information security education model. In: Miloslavskaya N., et al. (Eds.): Proc. of the 4th World Conf. on InfoSec Education (WISE-4). Moscow (2005) 22-35.
6. Krause M., Tipton F. 2006. Handbook of Information Security Management, CRC Press.
7. Morneau K.: Designing an Information Security Program as a core competency of Network Technologists. In: Proc. of the 5th Conf. on IT Education. ACM Press, USA (2004) 29-32.
8. Redwine S. (Ed.): Secure Software Assurance: A guide to the Common Body of Knowledge to produce, acquire and sustain secure software, US Dept. of Homeland Security (2006).
9. Slay J., Lock P.: Developing an Undergraduate IT Security Stream: Industry Certification and the Development of Graduate Qualities. In: Miloslavskaya N., et al. (Eds.): Proc. of the 4th World Conf. on Information Security Education (WISE-4). Moscow (2005) 57-66.
10. Smith E., Kritzinger E., Oostuizen H., Von Solms S.: Information Security education: Bridging the gap between academic institutions and industry. In: Miloslavskaya N., et al. (Eds.): Proc. of the 4th World Conf. on InfoSec Education (WISE-4). Moscow (2005) 45-55.
11. von Solms S.: Information Security - A Multidimensional Discipline. Computer & Security Vol. 20, No. 20. Elsevier (2001) 504-508.
12. Wilson M., Hash J.: Building an Information Technology Security Awareness and Training Program. NIST Special Publication 800-50. USA (2003).
13. Cresson-Wood C.: Why information security is now multi-disciplinary, multi-departmental, and multi-organizational in nature. Computer Fraud & Security, Elsevier (2004) 16-17.

A Course on Computer and Network Security: Teaching Online Versus Face-to-Face

Suresh Kalathur, Lubomir T. Chitkushev, Stuart Jacobs,
Tanya Zlateva, and Anatoly Temkin

Department of Computer Science, Metropolitan College, Boston University,
808 Commonwealth Avenue, Room 250, Boston, MA 02215, USA
{kalathur,ltc,sjjacobs,zlateva,temkin}@bu.edu

Abstract. The paper presents an overview of the Computer and Network Security course offered through distance education division as part of the online degree program. Topics presented in the online format are compared with those presented in a traditional curriculum in the face-to-face format. The pros and cons of each of the formats are discussed. Unique to the online course are weekly discussion topics that require each student's participation and the follow-ups to postings of other students. A distinguishing aspect of the online course is a three week based case study assignment exploring a practical security framework encountered in real companies.

Keywords: Computer security, network security, software security, distance education.

1   Introduction

Computer and network security is one of the fastest growing fields in information technology that poses a two-fold challenge to the educator: i) designing curricula that reflect the inter-disciplinary aspects of information security and integrate fields as diverse as technology, law, economics, management, policy, and ethics; and ii) finding delivery formats that make information security education widely available and at high quality. Online education is *the* fastest growing segment of the educational and training sector. It has firmly entered the mainstream: more than 3 million students were enrolled in at least one online course in 2005 as compared to 2.3 million in 2004 and this trend is expected to continue [1-2]. This evolution has led some researchers to describe online learning as a revolution in the nature of higher education that will result in a radical transformation from the currently predominant teacher-centered, face-to-face pedagogy to an online and hybrid, student-centered approach [3]. But even if one does not embrace the new delivery format, one can hardly overstate its importance and implications for the development of the workforce. This brings the question of the quality of online education—both its perception as well as actual documented learning outcomes—front and center in the discussion of new educational technologies. A growing number of publications are devoted to educational technologies that are based on the inherent characteristics of the new medium, espe-

Please use the following format when citing this chapter:

Kalathur, S., Chitkushev, L., Jacobs, S., Zlateva, T., Temkin, A., 2007, in IFIP International Federation for Information Processing, Volume 237, Fifth World Conference on Information Security Education, eds. Futcher, L., Dodge, R., (Boston: Springer), pp. 57–64.

cially multimedia, collaborative learning environments, learning networks, simulations and gaming [4].

This paper presents our experience with teaching a computer and network security course in an online delivery format, and striving to meet the demands of a highly technical, interdisciplinary subject in the context of the possibilities and limitations of the online medium. The course is part of the online MS CIS with concentration in information security. Boston University's information security programs [5] are nationally certified by CNNS and the University is recognized as a Center of Academic Excellence in Information Assurance Education. We have extensive experience with various distance education modes, more specifically we have offered videoconferencing courses (1996-2000), blended programs [6], and have currently one of the largest online graduate programs in security with over 300 students enrolled.

As part of our security curriculum, we offer the core course on computer and network security in both the face-to-face and online formats. The face-to-face course, on average, has approximately 20 students in each offering. The online classes, on the other hand, have an enrollment of approximately 120 – 150 students in each offering. The lecture materials for the online course are prepared by the instructor well in advance and exported by instructional designers into the online courseware system. During each course offering, the online course is divided into sections of 15 students each. A facilitator is assigned to each section and is solely responsible for the smooth running of that section, taking care of day-to-day interaction with the students, grading the assignments, monitoring the discussions, and providing timely feedback. The instructor assigned to the course oversees the facilitators and provides guidance and instructions to the facilitators in order to ensure uniform criteria are applied across all the sections by the various facilitators. Another major distinction between the two formats is the fact that the face-to-face course spans a 14 week period, whereas the online course runs during a 7 week time frame.

With face-to-face instruction there are a number of advantages – the instructor is able to take advantage of student *body language*, communication with students occurs in *real-time* as a dialogue, corrections may be rapidly disseminated, and the lecture material can be expanded upon extemporaneously and presented to all students immediately. However face-to-face instruction has some disadvantages – lecture material has to be preplanned to fit within a fixed class period time window, student attention during a class period may not be optimal, and student attendance may be prevented due to non-academic forces.

On the other hand, fixed class durations necessitate careful consideration of what, and how much, material will fit into the available time. This reality may impact the logical flow from subject to subject. Another reality of set class schedules is that a class may be scheduled at a time when a student's attention span is not optimal, such as in the evening after a student has already spent the day at their full time place of employment. If a student has no time for a break between work and class, then he/she can easily miss a meal or attend to other pressing activities. Given that students have non-academic responsibilities, these obligations can cause a student to miss a class. Lecture notes, or slides, are not as comprehensive as textbooks and typically serve as talking points for the instructor's lecture. So by missing a class, the student is unable to hear what the instructor presents in class, and being able to obtain the notes for the missed class does not fully make up for having missed the instructor's actual presentation. With the *distance/online* instruction, a student is able to choose when the best time is for reviewing the lecture material and is in a position to work around non-academic obligations.

2 Online Curriculum

The online course, *Computer and Network Security for Business* (MET CS695), is a required course for the students in the security concentration of the Master's program in Computer Information Systems. Prior to taking this course, students take the *Business Data Communications and Networks* (MET TC625) course as a prerequisite.

The following subsections describe in detail the contents covered during each week of the course. Aside from the lecture material provided to the students, communication amongst the students is strongly encouraged through weekly discussion topics. Assignments for each week ensure that the students do not lag in the study material for the week. The references listed in [7-11] are the primary materials referenced in the both the online and face-to-face courses.

2.1 Introduction and Security Overview

The material presented during the first week gives a bird's eye view of the security landscape from the perspective of a computer user – why is the user important to computer security, what are the threats to the user's computer, and as a user, what remedies are available. The notion of *defense, deterrence,* and *detection* and how they complement each other along with the controls and strategies required for a comprehensive security policy are then detailed. The *Common Body of Knowledge* and its domains and briefly explored during this lecture. Application security vulnerabilities are discussed with specific examples that include *SQL Injection, Cross-site scripting* and *buffer overflow* problems and case studies like the SQL Slammer, W32/Sobig.F worm, and W32/Blaster worm and their devastating capabilities are shown to the students.

2.2 Access Control and Operating System Security

The topics covered during this week include the security protection offered by the operating system itself. The address protection methods like fence registers, base and bound registers, segmentation, and paging techniques are explored here. Access control is then introduced from the perspective of a *reference monitor*. The concept of a subject, an object, and the access operations are illustrated.

Access control structures are then explored from an abstract viewpoint of the access control matrix and concrete implementations like the access control lists and the capability lists. The *Bell-LaPadula* security model for the confidentiality and the *Biba* model for the integrity of the data are shown. The *Chinese-Wall* model is then illustrated to handle the situations so that no conflicts of interest would ever occur in the system. Lastly, the *Clark-Wilson* model is shown in preserving the integrity within commercial applications.

The last lesson in this week's content presents the first half of the operating system security topics that include UNIX security and a practical illustration of role based access control in the *Solaris* operating system. Topics including user and group accounts, *setuid* and *setgid* attributes, and audit logs that record the security related events are explored.

2.3   Windows Security, Application Security, and Cryptography

A majority of the students work with Microsoft Windows based operating system and hence it is equally important to educate the students with the various aspects of Windows security. Starting with the Windows security architecture, the access control model is shown in terms of the *access tokens* and the *security descriptors*. The *discretionary access control list* and the *system access control list* (SACL) are shown with examples. The role of the *trust relationships* and *active directory* and the mechanisms to define them are depicted with real examples. The lesson on Windows security is wrapped up with a case study of how the *role-based access control* is set up in Windows Server 2003 and its distinction from the group-based access control.

The second lesson during this week's lecture material focuses on the buffer overruns resulting from poor coding practices, lack of safe string handling functions, stack and heap overruns, array indexing errors, etc. With the help of a few simple "C" programs, the above problems are demonstrated step by step and the outcomes before and after the problem code in question is executed are presented.

The next lesson primarily takes the *Java* programming language as the basis and presents the various security aspects from the perspective of the language itself. This week concludes with the lesson on the cryptographic functions and their uses. Public and private key encryption, confidentiality and authentication, substitution and transposition, mono alphabetic and poly alphabetic ciphers, DES and AES, RSA, message digest and fingerprints are thoroughly presented with examples.

After the first three weeks, the mid term exam is administered and then the curriculum proceeds with the network security part. The Network Security portion has been divided in three areas, each covering a week of online content. Our general idea was to start with the introduction of network security principles and authentication techniques, followed by network layer security framework and firewalls, and concluded by higher layers security protocols.

2.4   Network Security Principles and Authentication Protocols

The first week of network security (NS) covers the following topics: Rational for NS; Objectives for NS; Overview of Network Architectures (OSI and Internet Network model); NS Issues; Security of network layers; Security threats, risks, safeguards and vulnerability; Network threats and safeguards (covering LAN, WLAN, MAN, WAN and the Internet); NS services and mechanisms; Models of NS; Authentication protocols (Kerberos and X.509 Authentication service). Discussion topics for this section focus on key security concepts, such as security implications of centralizations based on key distribution schemas using an access control center or key distribution center. Other topics discussed are related to the ethics of network security, such as how should a CSO relate to vulnerabilities, both in the products used and in the products created by the company. Also how should the manufacturer (hardware and software) act when confronted with vulnerabilities found in their products are discussed.

2.5   Network Layer Security

The second week of material covers Network layer security framework, namely, the IP security framework; IPSec implementations; security associations; Key management and firewalls. In this section, the students learn about the challenges of providing security in a connectionless IP environment and the specific techniques used in the IPSec framework. Discussion topics for this week cover questions related to firewalls, such as why the firewalls should be configured to inspect both outgoing and incoming traffic. Also, they cover questions related to IPv6 such as whether the adoption of IPv6 in a near time would be more of a boost or a hindrance to security. Also how should a company approach the migration, and whether it will be additional burden on the company when time comes to adopt IPv6 are discussed.

2.6   Higher Layers Security

The last week of the network security part of the online course covers security of the transport and application layers. The topics covered are: SSL and TLS; Web security and Email security; and Secure electronic transactions (SET). The intent of this section is to expose the students in a systematic way to the main security protocols used for communication at the transport layer, and the advantages and ways of providing application layer security.

Discussion topics for this section focus on the advances made in application level security, and the fact that despite them we are still quite vulnerable to spamming and phishing, which costs the industry and the end-user millions of dollars each year. The students are asked to discuss what the weak points are and what would they suggest be done about them.

3   Face-to-Face Curriculum

The course, *Network and Software Security* (MET CS654), is offered every semester in the traditional face-to-face instruction. The following sections describe our face-to-face approach to the subject of information security. This course places the classic subjects of computer and communications security into the context of an over-arching security governance program and spans the major security knowledge domains in the Common Body of Knowledge recognized by the International Information Systems Security Certification Consortium (ISC).

3.1 Introduction to Information Security and Computer Security Concepts

These lectures (over a 4 week period) begin with business drivers, security policies, security domains, and security models. Vulnerabilities, formal threat concepts and basic attack concepts are then presented along with taxonomies of threats, threat agents, and attacks. An overview of the concepts of security services and security mechanisms is presented followed with a review of cryptography concepts (symmetric & asymmetric encryption, keyed hashes, digital signatures, and cryptanalysis). Also covered are protection in Operation Systems (OS), OS memory security mechanisms, user authentication and protection of passwords, and the need for file system security. OS security layers/rings are presented with details on OS Security controls. A review of basic networking concepts (protocols, routing and network types) and current security mechanisms/capabilities by protocol concludes this section.

3.2 Security of Specific Operating Systems

These lectures (over a 4 week period) present security within typical operating systems, namely: UNIX security, UNIX Best Practices, Linux Security, Solaris OS & Role Based Access Control (RBAC), Embedded OS Security, and Windows. Database management systems (DBMS) security is discussed along with the application of Clark-Wilson concepts to DBMS. The following lectures consider the application of encypherment for the following areas – authentication (symmetric, asymmetric, hashes), confidentiality (symmetric, asymmetric), integrity (symmetric, hashes), non-repudiation (asymmetric), and conclude with a discussion on key management (KDCs-Kerberos, PKI-Digital Certificates, Key Distribution Keys vs. Session Keys).

3.3 Networking Security Mechanisms and Security Management

These lectures (over a 4 week period) begin with a discussion of current authentication, confidentiality & integrity deficiencies within protocol layers. Mechanisms to mitigate networking vulnerabilities are presented including: IEEE 802.1x, IPsec, TLS-DTLS-SSL, SSH, firewalls, application gateways, deep packet inspection, network application security (e.g., Email, VoIP), and the usefulness of XML security mechanisms. A series of network security use cases are presented (ISP, Enterprise, and Service Provider) to demonstrate the layering of the aforementioned security mechanisms. The final lecture tackles the issue of managing deployed security mechanisms from a TMN Model perspective and then focuses in on Security Service Management (Security Event-Fault-Attack Management, Security Configuration Management, Login Access Management, Authentication Credentials Management, and Verification and Validation Management).

4   Assessments

In the case of the face-to-face course, students are evaluated through a set of homework problems, a mid term exam, a final exam, and student participation through the duration of the course. The online course, on the other hand, has weekly discussion topics, weekly assignment problems, a mid term exam, and a final proctored exam. The discussion topics for each week are prepared in advance by the instructor. Participation is graded based on the student's contribution to the original topic and as well as their follow up postings on other students' postings. The mid term exam, in most part, consists of a series of short paragraph style questions, and students have a fixed duration of 3 hours from the time they start the assessment at any time during the mid term exam week. The final exam is a proctored 3 hour exam, proctored at an authorized test site, or through a designated proctor when a test site is unavailable within a reasonable geographic distance.

A notable feature of the online class for the network security portion is a 3-week single assignment, with deliverables expected in each of the three weeks. The students are required to develop a case study and submit a report in the form of a short paper exploring the points requested. When developing the case study the students are free to use the material covered in the lectures, textbook as well as other sources that have to be mentioned in the bibliography. Each weekly assignment is worth the same number of points.

During the first week the students are asked to assume the role of a CSOs (Chief Security Officers) for a newly formed company (such as a bio-technology start-up) The students are given the main information about the structure of the company and their international divisions, as well as the work process requirements pertaining to data stored in its internal network. For the first week the students are required to provide a rationale for the level of security they think should be enforced. They are required to give a topology of the suggested network and explain the choices made, and characterize the protocols (both transport and application) present in the suggested topology, and the rational for selecting them.

During the second week the students are required to provide a threat assessment report for the internal network(s) of the company as defined in the first assignment, and point the mechanisms used to mitigate these threats, and where they'll be used. They can also include any other form of security prevention measure (choice of OS, hardware, vendor, etc.).

During the third week the students are required to refine the second week's work by adding application-level security. Also, students have to analyze security threats and address each of them, by proposing an appropriate security mechanism. The three weekly portions of the assignment form a logical sequence that enables students to learn the subject through applied exercises of increasing complexity, and have been positively mentioned in student evaluations.

5   Conclusion

In the above sections, we presented the topics presented to the students in the on-line program versus the face-to-face course. The course evaluation for the face-to-face program currently uses different criteria from the online program. We are in the process of developing a uniform set of student assessment criteria for both these programs. In the face-to-face course, the instructor is solely responsible for the success of the course. In the case of our online program, the facilitators along with the instructor play a crucial role in maintaining the day-to-day interaction and meeting the expectations of a wider body of students. By developing a richer assortment of interactive modules, the satisfaction rate of the online students can be significantly increased. All these components, otherwise unavailable to the face-to-face instructor and the students, can be incorporated into the traditional curriculum and provide a greater experience to their audience as well.

References

1. Allen, E.; Seaman, J.: Entering the Mainstream: The Quality and Extent of Online Education in the United States, 2003-2004. Sloan Center for Online Education at Olin and Babson College, Needham, MA 2004.
2. Allen, E.; Seaman, J.: Making the Grade: Online Education in the United States 2006. Sloan Center for Online Education at Olin and Babson College, Needham, MA 2006.
3. Hiltz, S.R.; Turoff, M.: The Evolution of Online Learning and the Revolution in Higher Education. Communication of the ACM, October 2005, vol. 48, No. 10.
4. Hiltz, S.R.; Goldman, R. (Eds): Learning Together Online: Research on Asynchronous Learning Networks. Erlbaum, Mahwah, NJ, 2005.
5. Zlateva, S.; Kanabar, V.; Temkin, A., Citkusev, L.T.; Kalathur, S: Integrated Curricula for Computer and Network Security Education, Proceedings of the Colloquium for Information Systems Security Education, Society for Advancing Information Assurance and Infrastructure Protection, Washington, D.C., June 3-5, 2003.
6. Zlateva, T.; J. Burstein: "A Web-Based Graduate Certificate for IT Professionals - Design Choices and First Evaluation Results". Proceedings of the 2001 Annual Conference of the American Society for Engineering Education(ASEE), June 24-27, Albuquerque, New Mexico.
7. Anderson, R.: Security Engineering: A Guide to Building Dependable Distributed Systems. Wiley, 2001.
8. Gollmann, D.: Computer Security, 2nd edition. Wiley, 2006.
9. Howard, M. and LeBlanc, D.: Writing Secure Code, 2nd edition. Microsoft Press, 2002.
10. Stallings, W.: Network Security Essentials: Applications and Standards, 3rd edition. Prentice-Hall, 2007.
11. Charlie Kaufman, Radia Perlman and Mike Speciner, *Network Security -- Private Communication in a Public World, 2nd Edition*, Prentice-Hall, 2002.

An Interdisciplinary Approach to Forensic IT and Forensic Psychology Education

Clare Wilson[1], Vasilios Katos[2], Caroline Strevens[3]

[1] Department of Psychology, University of Portsmouth, UK
[2] School of Computing, University of Portsmouth, UK
[3] Department of Accounting and Law, University of Portsmouth, UK
{clare.wilson, vasilios.katos, caroline.strevens}@port.ac.uk

Abstract. In WISE 4, Armstrong [1] presented a multidisciplinary view in computer forensics education. The view was primarily focusing solely on the education of computer forensics students, which was indeed along the lines of multidisciplinarity. However, this view does not involve integration between the different disciplines. In this paper, the scope of the approach is extended in order to allow a two- or three-way relationship between the disciplines of Computing, Psychology and Law and thus create an interdisciplinary perspective. It is shown how the study material was integrated and developed to suit the three disciplines.

Keywords: computer forensics, forensic psychology, expert testimony.

1 Introduction

Both multidisciplinarity and interdisciplinarity have received in recent years a significant amount of attention not only in the area of security education, but in a variety of fields. For example, Browne [2] discusses the impact of an interdisciplinary approach to environmental education and Gardner *et al.* [3] address the relevant needs in healthcare. With respect to security education, Gritzalis *et al.* [4] present a detailed analysis towards developing an interdisciplinary model for information security education.

It is argued that a multidisciplinary approach is not sufficient in forensic education, due to the nature of forensics. The main reason is that forensic science is in its minimum a bi-disciplinary subject, encompassing a scientific component and a legal component. Yasinsac *et al.* [5] categorically identify that a computer forensic scientist must have a background in Computer Science, Law and Forensics. Furthermore, the forensic analysis process operates in an open and complex problem space, due to the increased uncertainty. If for instance a forensic investigation refers to an activity attributed to an individual or a group of people, psychology would play an important role.

Interdisciplinarity on the other hand refers to the integration of different perspectives into an epistemological identity [4]. For a forensic investigator, learning to manage and work across many disciplines is indeed a critical success factor. This

Please use the following format when citing this chapter:

Wilson, C., Katos, V., Stevens, C., 2007, in IFIP International Federation for Information Processing, Volume 237, Fifth World Conference on Information Security Education, eds. Futcher, L., Dodge, R., (Boston: Springer), pp. 65–71.

can be easily established if the forensic investigation is viewed as a research process; in research, many of the intellectual breakthroughs were made by crossing disciplinary boundaries [6]. An explanation to Morillo's et al. statement can be found in Barker *et al.* [7], who reason that researchers make valuable contributions to fields outside of their specialty by asking questions from a different viewpoint, as opposed to the narrower perspective of the "insiders" of the field.

The above setting is prevalent in computer forensics. For example, a suspect hard disk may host encrypted data and the path to decrypting the data (assuming that all cryptanalytic attacks have failed and the only option left is exhaustive search) is usually to construct a case specific dictionary, to mount a dictionary attack. The psychology of the suspect may aid the investigation, for example, offender profiling may indicate certain tastes and preferences in the suspect which may help in constructing a candidate list of passwords. Similarly, information obtained from the analysis of the digital evidence may contribute to the understanding of the socio-psychological behaviour of the suspect.

The rest of this paper is structured as follows. In Section 2 there is a brief discussion of the MSc programmes in Forensic IT and Forensic Psychology taught at the University of Portsmouth. Section 3 describes the forensic process exercise, as it spawns between the two disciplines and concludes with the mock trial involving the law students from the Department of Accounting and Law. Section 4 presents lessons learned and areas for further development.

2 Forensic IT and Forensic Psychology

The structure of the MSc in Forensic IT is depicted in Fig. 1. Albeit exhibiting a modular approach, all modules are stemming from the "Digital Forensics" module. More precisely, the process of acquisition, preservation, analysis and reporting is covered by the digital forensics unit, but the more advanced skills required to perform the individual processes are covered by the supporting modules of cryptography, offender profiling, network security, data mining, white collar crime, cyber crime and strategic risk management.

The MSc in Forensic Psychology is also a modular design, all integrated to examine the criminal behaviour, investigation, prosecution and treatment of offenders. One module, Psychology and Investigations, was dedicated to the examination of the same case module used in the Digital Forensics module of the MSc in Forensic IT.

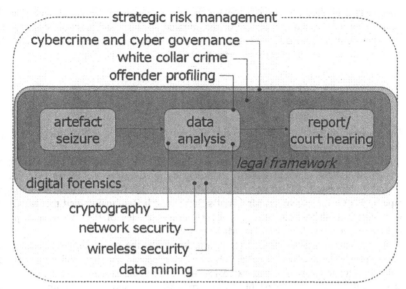

Fig. 1. The MSc in Forensic IT structure

2.1 The digital forensics laboratory

The Digital Forensics Lab (DFL) is a specialised, state of the art laboratory, enabling the students undertaking the digital forensics and network security module (which primarily focuses on the network forensics aspects), to gain practical, hands on experience on forensic discovery of digital storage media.

The DFL is equipped with both open source and commercial software and specialist hardware (such as hardware blockers, hardware bitstream copying devices). The lab consists of three rooms: the main teaching room, the evidence room which contains lockable cabinets where the students are assigned keys for accessing the evidence, and the production room which hosts the servers and network equipment.

The lab is self sustained, with two networks, namely the attack network and the forensic network. The former is used for studying network security related issues, such as denial of service attacks, vulnerability scanning, code injection etc. It is envisaged that in the longer run it will be able to regularly participate in cyber security exercises (see for example Dodge *et al.* [8]). The latter network allows limited access to the internet, which is needed in order to complete certain tasks.

Students use the lab to study digital forensics, cryptography and network security. Due to the nature of the course, the forensic students have exclusive access to the lab and are required to subscribe to a code of ethics. The lab complies with certain requirements relating to forensic investigations (swipe card access, no windows, and no false ceilings). Furthermore, the students have limited technical support and in effect have the "ownership" of the lab; they have administrative access to the computers and they are responsible for the maintenance of the equipment. This is required as it is a vital component of the adopted teaching and learning strategy and furthermore this responsibility is part of the skills they need to acquire in order to be prepared to face real life scenarios once they graduate from the course.

3   The Module Delivery Process

The case study was jointly developed by the Department of Psychology and the School of Computing of the University of Portsmouth.

The case involved the alleged rape and murder of a student, Ms Ima Meanie (a woman with Dissociative Identity Disorder) by a computer technician, Mr Gil T. Ornot. A depressed student associate of Ms Meanie, Ms Clare-Lee Blue also alleged rape by Mr Ornot. However, Mr Ornot's flatmate, Ali Bye, maintained that Mr Ornot was with him the whole time. However, computer files of the case can disprove statements made by Mr Ornot and Mr Bye.

A disk image was developed reflecting aspects of the chronology of events. The key digital evidence was a collection of photographs, chat logs and an encrypted volume. The latter was a bad extension file, where the students were required to examine the file header to establish the correct file type and proceed with recovering the evidence.

The digital investigation process was initiated by a search warrant (Fig. 2), requiring the students to form a team led by a nominated team member. Prior activities, apart from the technical training on forensic tools such as the Forensic Tool Kit and The Sleuth Kit with its front end (Autopsy), included the development of the relevant evidence forms, such as a Chain of Custody form and a Multi Evidence Form, as well as a documented, formal description of the evidence seizure process.

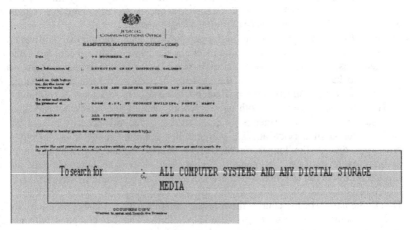

Fig. 2. The search warrant

The digital forensics team was equipped with the following equipment to handle the evidence discovered at the crime scene:

- cameras
- laptops with hardware write blockers
- evidence bags
- hardware forensic bit stream copying devices, capable of computing the MD5 and SHA-1 hashes of the acquired hard disks.

During the seizure all team members had clear roles and responsibilities assigned by the leader. The role allocation was performed prior to visiting the crime scene, as there was a briefing from the leader. The role allocation process considered the four Association of Chief Police Officers (ACPO) principles [9] and therefore the individual's expertise was taken into account.

Interdisciplinarity is further enforced with a formal meeting between the forensic psychologists and the computer forensics investigators, to exchange discovered information and consolidate findings. The psychologists were particularly interested in the timestamps of the digital files, in order to verify the chronology of events and establish whether the suspect lied during their testify statement. The forensic investigators were interested in understanding the personality attributes of the suspect, in order to narrow down the cryptanalytic attack to the encrypted files. The fact alone that certain files may be encrypted, as well as the type of the encrypted content in turn provided valuable information both to the psychologists and lawyers.

3.1. The path to court

In a criminal trial it is for the jury to decide on the facts proven. However they can be helped in this task with expert evidence. An expert is entitled to give an opinion only on relevant matters which are within his particular area of expertise and which are outside the general knowledge and understanding of the jury.

"[O]ne purpose of jury trials is to bring into the jury box a body of men and women who are able to judge ordinary day-to-day questions by their own standards, … Where the matters in issue go outside that experience and they are invited to deal with someone supposedly abnormal, for example, supposedly suffering from insanity or diminished responsibility, then plainly in such a case they are entitled to the benefit of expert evidence." (R v Chard (1971) 56 Cr App R 268 (CA) pp 270 -1)

It was confirmed in R v Mackenney (No.2) 2004 2 Cr App R 32 that expert evidence is admissible on the reliability of the accused or some other witness testimony only if the evidence suggests a medical abnormality. Otherwise it is not admissible.

In the Crown court the judge, at the plea and case management hearing will make directions about whether expert evidence is to be obtained and if so what. The prosecution must serve expert testimony in report form on the defence before the trial starts. The defence must respond by submitting a Defence Case Statement setting out the general nature of the defence and what differences there are with the prosecution.

If the accused intends to rely on an alibi, further details must be served on the prosecution to enable them to bring evidence to refute this.

Thus it is apparent that the lawyers involved must be briefed on the technical aspects of expert testimony before they can advise on its admissibility or on the steps necessary to challenge it. In the case study it was decided only to involve the law students in the delivery of the evidence at trial rather than in its preparation and exchange (although it is planned to do so in subsequent academic years in conjunction with the delivery of a Law of Evidence module on the Legum Baccalaureus (LLB) or Batchelor of Law degree). In the case study law students were paired with psychology and forensics students in order for that briefing before the trial was to take place. The law students had to understand the technical issues in order to formulate the outcomes for the cross-examination and to prepare their questions.

An expert must be skilled in matters about which he is asked to give an opinion. He has an over-riding duty to help the court on the matter which overrides any obligation to the party from whom he received instructions. The expert must thus state his qualifications and experience in his evidence and will be open to cross-examination on this point. The expert must state in his report the main points of all written instructions given to him. This is in order to prevent the parties from asking the expert to change his conclusion. Any discrepancies will also be an area for cross-examination.

Although it is ultimately for the jury to decide the expert may give his opinion on the likely innocence or guilt of the accused.

The forensics students presented evidence as to the contents of the hard drive of the accused. They had to brief the law students on the authenticity of the materials found, and explain how any deleted files were recovered in secure form so that they could give evidence that there was no possibility of tampering by another person after the computer was seized.

4 Conclusions

In this paper an interdisciplinary approach for developing and delivering educational material for teaching forensic computing students and forensic psychologists, with the view of involving law students was presented.

The forensic students, both in psychology and computing, developed an appreciation for their peer forensic investigators and understood that integrating two disciplines on an epistemological level not only results in added value from an educational perspective, but also that it is of a paramount importance that forensic discovery involves different specialists in order to compensate for the significant uncertainty that governs the forensic analysis process.

The law students gained a valuable opportunity to learn a little more about the criminal justice process (outside the curriculum at undergraduate level – normally learned on a Legal Practice Course, LPC or a Bar Vocational Course, BVC) and to hone their communication and advocacy skills. Although law students are used to Mooting, which involves presenting arguments on points of law, they do not often gain the experience of cross-examination.

References

1. Armstrong, C., 2005, Computer Forensics Education – A Multi-Discipline View, WISE 4 Proceedings, Moscow, 18-20 May, pp.205-212.
2. Browne, M., 2002, The Mandate for Interdisciplinarity in Science Education: The Case of Economic and Environmental Sciences, Science & Education, 11, pp.513-522.
3. Gardner, S. Chamberlin, G., Heestad, D., Stowe, C., 2002, Interdisciplinary Didactic Instruction at Academic Health Centers in the United States: Attitudes and Barriers. Advances in Health Sciences Education, 7, pp. 179-190.
4. Gritzalis, D., Theoharidou, M., Kalimeri, E. 2005, Towards an Interdisciplinary Information Security Education Model., WISE 4 Proceedings, Moscow, 18-20 May, pp.22-35.
5. Yasinsac, A., Erbacjer, F., Marks, G., Pollitt, M., Sommer, M., 2003, Computer Forensics Education, IEEE Security and Privacy, 1(4) pp. 15-23.
6. Morillo, F., Bordons, M., Gomez, I., 2003, Interdisciplinarity in Science: A Tentative Typology of Disciplines and Research Areas, Journal of the Americal Society for Information Science and Technology, 54(13), pp.1237-1249.
7. Barker, R., Gilbreath, G., Stone, W. 1998, The Interdisciplinary needs of Organisations: Are New Employees Adequately Equipped?, Journal of Management Development, 17(3), pp.219-232.
8. Dodge, R., Hoffman, L., Ragsdale, D., Rosenberg, T., 2005, Exploring a Cyber Security Exercise, WISE 4 Proceedings, Moscow, 18-20 May, pp.94-101.
9. Association of Chief Police Officers (ACPO), Good Practice Guide for Computer based Electronic Evidence, National High Tech Crime Unit. Available at: http://www.acpo.police.uk/asp/policies/Data/gpg_computer_based_evidence_v3.pdf

Experiences from Educating Practitioners in Vulnerability Analysis

Stefan Lindskog, Hans Hedbom, Leonardo A. Martucci, and
Simone Fischer-Hübner

Department of Computer Science
Karlstad University, SE-651 88 Karlstad, Sweden
{stefan.lindskog|hans.hedbom|leonardo.martucci|simone.fischer-huebner}
@kau.se

Abstract. This paper presents a vulnerability analysis course especially developed for practitioners and experiences gained from it. The described course is a compact three days course initially aimed to educate practitioners in the process of finding security weaknesses in their own products. After giving an overview of the course, the paper presents results from two different types of course evaluations. One evaluation was done on-site at the last day of the course, while the other was made 3–18 months after the participants had finished the course. Conclusions drawn from it with regard to recommended content for vulnerability analysis courses for practitioners are also provided.

1   Introduction

The ongoing trend of a growing number of security vulnerabilities, threats and incidents has increased the efforts of IT industry to invest in the development of more secure systems. Vulnerability analysis (VA) is an important mean for improving security assurance of IT systems during test and integration phases. The approach that VA takes is to find weaknesses of the security of a system or parts of the system. These potential vulnerabilities are assessed through penetration testing to determine whether they could, in practice, be exploitable to compromise the security of the system. The Common Criteria have requirements on VA to be performed for the evaluation of systems with an Evaluation Assurance Level 2 (EAL2) or higher [2].

Upon request by a major IT company, our Department developed a compact VA course to be held on three working days for an international and heterogeneous, in terms of knowledge in the security area, group of practitioners from industry. Experiences and lessons learned from supervised student penetration testing experiments within an applied computer security course held at our Department [5] provided us with some inputs for the preparation of this VA course.

The emphasis of our VA course developed for industry was put on practical, hands-on experiments. The course outline and first experiences gained from the course held in 2005 were first presented in [6]. Meanwhile, after the course has been held at our department five times with an average number of 16 participants

Please use the following format when citing this chapter:

Lindskog, S., Hedbom, H., Martucci, L., Fischer-Hübner, S., 2007, in IFIP International Federation for Information Processing, Volume 237, Fifth World Conference on Information Security Education, eds. Futcher, L., Dodge, R., (Boston: Springer), pp. 73–80.

in 2005 and 2006, we were interested in a more detailed evaluation by means of a statistical survey. Our aim was to investigate how useful the participants have perceived the practical experiments and course content for their jobs, what influence it has had on their work, and whether they think that the course has helped to improve the overall quality of the test procedures applied by their companies. The results of this survey and conclusions drawn from it with regard to the recommended content of compact VA courses for IT industry will be presented in this paper.

The rest of the paper is organized as follows. Section 2 gives a brief overview of the course and its content. Especially the hands-on assignments are presented. In Section 3, the on-site course evaluation is discussed, whereas Section 4 describe the results achieved from the post course evaluation performed. Experiences from the course and conclusions are provided in Section 5.

2 Course Overview

This section will give a brief description of the course. A more thorough discussion can be found in [6]. The requested course was initially aimed for software testers with no or little knowledge about security in general and VA in particular, but with an extensive knowledge in software testing. However, as will be discussed later, in reality the participants had a more diversified background and very few actually worked as testers. Since the target group was practitioners, a practical course was requested. Approximately 1/3 of the course cover theoretical aspects and 2/3 is used for practical hands-on assignments. The latter was intended to give the attendees hands-on experience on how to conduct a VA of either a software component or a complete system. A three days course (24 hours course) was selected as the best choice for the course length, since the participants should not be absent from their tasks for a long period. The course is divided into the four following blocks: (1) introduction to computer and network security, (2) computer and network security protocols and tools, (3) VA, and (4) known vulnerabilities, reconnaissance tools, and information gathering. The following 10 hands-on assignments are provided in the course:

1. **Password cracking with John the Ripper.** In this experiment, a local password cracker application is experienced. John the Ripper v.1.6, a password cracker tool, which is intended to detect weak UNIX passwords [11] is used. This tool is both easy to use and easy to deploy. Synthetic (artificially populated) passwd and shadow files from a Linux box is provided.
2. **Testing for randomness using the NIST test suite.** In this experiment, the NIST Statistical Test Suite [8] is used to evaluate outputs from different pseudo random number generators (PRNG). It implements 15 statistical tests. It has also embedded implementations of well-known bad PRNG, such as the XOR RNG, and also NIST approved RNG, such as the ANSI X9.31. Sample data files are also provided as companion part of this test suite.
3. **Network sniffing using Ethereal.** The assignment is divided in two parts, each part with a different network topology. In the first part, the participants

verify that a popular network protocol, i.e., TELNET, is weak regarding security using a network analyzer tool [3]. In the second part, a rather insignificant change in the network topology is made that modified the test result and it is up to the participants to explain why the result changes.

4. **ARP spoofing using Cain & Abel.** In this assignment, the participants test an ARP spoofing tool [10] on a switched network, verify the achieved results, and explain the results accordingly.

5. **Black-box testing using the PROTOS tool.** In this experiment the PROTOS tool [12] is used as a black box testing tool against the SNMP protocol implementation of Cisco 1005 router running IOS 11.1(3). The PROTOS Test Suite c06-snmpv1 is here used to perform a Denial of Service (DoS) attack against the Cisco router.

6. **Firewall configuration.** This exercise is based on an assignment originally published in [7]. The participants are divided into groups of two. Each group is given a description of a setup and is asked to write firewall rules in Linux using ipTables implementing a given policy defined in the problem statement.

7. **Node hardening using Bastille.** Since the participants have a heterogeneous background regarding in-depth knowledge of different operating systems, the open source tool Bastille [1] is selected for the this assignment. The tool lets the user answer a number of questions on how they want the computer to be configured and then configures it according to the answers. The participants were asked to make their own computers as secure as possible given that they still should be functional as networked computers.

8. **Port scanning with NMAP.** The goal of this experiment is gathering information about two running systems. Two workstations configured as servers (one Linux and one Windows server) are used as target systems. The participants run the Network Mapper (NMAP) [4], an open source port scanning tool, under Linux. Servers run several network services, such as FTP, HTTP, NetBIOS, etc. The participants have to find and identify the servers in a given IP network range, since their IP addresses are not provided, find out the operating system running, and identify the open ports in each server

9. **Security scanning with NESSUS.** In this exercise, two target servers are set up. One Windows 2000 (set up as a domain server) and one running Fedora Core 3 Linux. None of the servers are patched, running all standard services and acting as target systems for the security scanner [9]. The participants are divided into pairs and they are asked to find the servers IP addresses and to find out which operating systems they are running. After finding the servers, the participants had to scan them and report all the vulnerabilities found.

10. **Final assignment (putting it all together).** The last assignment is a full-day final practical assignment that concludes the course, a "putting it all together" experiment that summarizes the full VA process. In this exercise, the participants are divided into groups of four. Each group is given a Fedora Core 3 Linux server with all services running. Every group also got

a requirement document describing the role of the server and the security requirements on it. They are asked to find out what needed to be done in order to fulfill the requirements and also to perform the changes and verify the results. In order to do this they had access to all the tools used in the previous exercises and a list of useful Internet links. They also had access to the Internet and are told that they could use it freely. Moreover, they may also use any other freely available tool found on Internet. The participants had to report all the miss-configured parameters, vulnerabilities and also had to suggest changes in the system in order to adhere to the specification. The results were discussed in a summing-up session just after the exercise.

3   On-Site Course Evaluation

In this section, we present the results from the on-site evaluation that was performed as the last activity within the course. The participants assessed the usefulness of the 10 assignments within the course. The questionnaires were answered individually and anonymously.

The main question regarding the evaluation of the assignments were formulated as follows: "*An important part of the course is the hands-on assignments. Please give your opinion about the usefulness of these using the 1–7 scale (1 means poor and 7 means excellent)*". The participants were encouraged to motivate their answer. Table 1 summarizes the result from the on-site evaluations. The results are presented in percentages of the total feedback for each assignment and the most likely grade, i.e., the statistical type value, is highlighted in boldface. The presented results were based on a total of 60 evaluations collected from the participants in five course instances from spring 2005 to autumn 2006.

Table 1: Results from the question: "Please give your opinion about the usefulness of the assignments using the 1–7 scale (1 means poor and 7 means excellent)".

Grade	Assignments									
	1	2	3	4	5	6	7	8	9	10
1				2%				2%		
2		16%			7%					3%
3		8%	5%	3%	7%	2%			2%	7%
4	11%	**24%**	10%	10%	25%	13%	10%	8%	3%	22%
5	39%	**24%**	27%	32%	25%	23%	22%	31%	23%	31%
6	**47%**	**24%**	**45%**	**42%**	**33%**	**47%**	**53%**	**47%**	**50%**	**32%**
7	3%	3%	13%	10%	3%	15%	15%	12%	22%	5%

The assignment considered the most useful by the participants was the security scanning using the NESSUS, followed by the port scanning assignment with NMAP. The least useful assignment, according to the on-site evaluation, was the test for randomness using the NIST tool. According to the feedback collected from the participants, the security and port scanning tools could be easily deployed and used during test phase, but testing for randomness was a fairly more uncommon and also a fairly slow test in comparison to the other assignments.

All the participants that have taken the course so far have either been satisfied or very satisfied. Additional results from the on-site evaluation is given in [6].

4   Post Course Evaluation

The post course evaluation was conducted in January 2007, which was 3–18 months after the participants had taken the course. The evaluation was performed based on a web based questionnaire. The prior participants were contacted by email to voluntarily provide their input within one week. All in all, 55 emails were sent out to prior course participants and 22 of them filled in the questionnaire. The questionnaire contained the following 12 questions:

1. *Position when the course was given*
2. *Number of years in that position*
3. *Current position*
4. *Country of residence*
5. *Education (Technical degree, Management degree, or Other)*
6. *Did the course fulfill your expectation? (Yes or No)*
7. *What is the most important learning outcome from the course?*
8. *To what degree have the course helped you in your position? (1 means not at all and 7 means very well)*
9. *An important part of the course is the hands-on assignments. In retrospect, please give your opinion about these using the 1-7 scale. (1 means poor and 7 means excellent)*
10. *Do you practically apply any of the tools/techniques from the assignments in your current position? (Never, Sometimes, or Often)*
11. *Do you think that the knowledge gained from the course has helped to improve the overall quality of the test procedures you apply? (Yes, No, or I don't know)*
12. *Other comments/suggestions*

The indent with the first question was to investigate the respondents' job positions when they took the course. Based on the input five main job categories could be distinguished (number of persons in each categories are specified within parenthesis): software tester (5.5^1), technical specialist (6) software engineer (3.5), system manager (4), and manager (3). To the manager category project, product, and platform managers are counted. The number of years in that position varied between 0 and 10 years. From question 3 we found that one software tester and one system engineer had advanced to a system manager position. The number of persons in the other two categories had not changed. From the country of residence question, we found that 2/3 of the respondents were from Sweden and the rest from abroad. These figures reflect the distribution of the participants that have taken the course. 20 out of 22, i.e., 91%, reported a technical degree and the other two in the other category. All 22 respondents answered that the course did fulfill their expectations. The most important learning

---

[1] One respondent reported a shared position as software tester and software engineer.

outcomes that were reported in the questionnaires are (1) knowledge about and experiences with the tools, and (2) awareness of security in general and VA in particular. The results from question 8 is illustrated in Fig. 1.

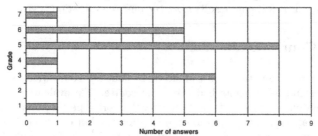

Fig. 1: Results from question 8: "To what degree have the course helped you in your position? (1 means not at all and 7 means very well)".

From the figure it is evident that more than 60% of the respondents reported that the course have helped them in their positions quite much, much, or very much (i.e., grade 5–7). The respondent that reported that the course has not at all helped was, at the time the course was taken, acting as a manager and is still in that position. Remember from Section 2 that the course was not targeted for that job category.

In question 9, the respondents were asked to give their opinions about the different assignments in retrospect. The result is presented in Table 2. The statistical type value is again highlighted in boldface.

Table 2: Results from question 9: "In retrospect, please give your opinion about the assignments using the 1-7 scale. (1 means poor and 7 means excellent)".

Grade	Assignments									
	1	2	3	4	5	6	7	8	9	10
1										
2	9%	23%			5%		9%		5%	
3	14%	5%		14%	5%			5%		9%
4	9%	**32%**	14%	14%	23%	18%	9%	23%	14%	18%
5	**32%**	18%	23%	**32%**	**32%**	32%	**41%**	**32%**	23%	18%
6	27%	23%	**50%**	**32%**	18%	**45%**	32%	23%	**41%**	**41%**
7	9%		14%	9%	18%	5%	9%	18%	18%	14%

From the table it is clear that the respondents were satisfied with all 10 assignments. The most popular assignments in retrospect were assignments 3 (network sniffing using Ethereal) and 6 (firewall configuration). Remember from Section 3 that these were not graded highest in the on-site evaluation. Instead, assignments 8 (port scanning with NMAP) and 9 (security scanning with NESSUS) were the most popular ones.

Question 10 was asked to investigate whether the participants have applied the tools/techniques used in the assignments professionally. The results are presented in Fig. 2. From the figure it is evident that knowledge gained from as-

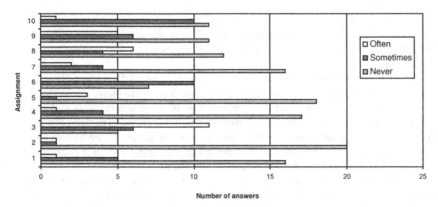

Fig. 2: Results from question 10: "Do you practically apply any of the tools/techniques from the assignments in your current position? (Never, Sometimes, or Often)".

signments 3 (Network sniffing using Ethereal) and 6 (Firewall configuration) are either used often or sometimes by 17 and 15 respondents, respectively. Hence, the tools used in these assignments are the ones that are used most frequently by the respondents after the course. This is probably also the reason why these assignments are graded highest in the previous question. Similarly, the least used tool reported by the respondents was the one introduced in assignment 2 (Testing for raddomness using the NIST test suite). This assignment was assigned the lowest grade of all 10 assignments in both the on-site and post evaluation.

In question 11, the respondents were asked whether they believe that the course has helped to improve the quality of the test procedures and 17 (i.e., more than 77%) answered "Yes". The remaining five respondents answered that they did not know.

5   Experiences and Conclusions

Our experience is that during a compact three days course in VA aimed for practitioners many different issues can be covered. The respondents from the post evaluation have reported that most of them are convinced that the knowledge gained from the course has helped them to produce products with higher quality than before. From the various instances of the course and through the on-site evaluations and the post evaluation, we have learned that the mixture of practical hands-on assignment during 2/3 of the time and lectures 1/3 of the time are suitable when educating practitioners in VA. We have also learned that the participants' opinion about assignments might change over time.

Assignment 2, i.e., testing for randomness using the NIST test suite, needs special attention. This assignment was added to the course on request from the contractor because of its importance for developing secure cryptographic systems. Based on the on-site evaluations and post evaluation very few of the participants have graded this assignment very high. In addition, only two of the respondents in the post evaluation have reported that they have used the knowledge from this assignment afterwards. Hence, for future course instances we plan to skip this exercise, but still cover the theory on testing for randomness in the course.

From both the on-site evaluations and post evaluation it is clear that the course has been appreciated by the participants. The course has, furthermore, steadily been changed based on the participants' invaluable comments and suggestions for enhancement, but also based on the lecturers feelings from the five different course instances so far conducted. Except assignment 2, we believe that the theory as well as the assignments covered in the course together provides a very well balanced VA course for practitioners. We also believe that the course, or at least parts of it, would fit nicely in the third year of Bachelor programs in computer science, computer engineering, or information technology.

On request form the contractor, and some of the course participants, a one day follow-up course is now under development. The follow-up course will focus on: wireless networks, authentication, authorization, and accounting (AAA) architectures, and virtual private networks (VPNs).

References

1. Bastille Linux. The Bastille hardening program: Increased security for your OS. http://www.bastille-linux.org/, Accessed January 23, 2007.
2. Common Criteria Implementation Board. Common criteria for information technology security evaluation, version 3.1. http://www.commoncriteriaportal.org/, September 2006.
3. Ethereal, Inc. Ethereal: A network protocol analyzer. http://www.ethereal.com, Accessed January 23, 2007.
4. Insecure.org. Network mapper. http://insecure.org/nmap/, Accessed January 23, 2007.
5. S. Lindskog, U. Lindqvist, and E. Jonsson. IT security research and education in synergy. In *Proceedings of the 1st World Conference in Information Security Education (WISE'1)*, pages 147–162, Stockholm, Sweden, June 17–19, 1999.
6. L. A. Martucci, H. Hedbom, S. Lindskog, and S. Fischer-Hübner. Educating system testers in vulnerability analysis: Laboratory development and deployment. In *Proceedings of the Seventh Workshop on Education in Computer Security (WECS'7)*, pages 51–65, Monterey, CA, USA, January 4–6, 2006.
7. Mixter. Gut behütet. *C'T – Magazin für Computer Technik*, pages 202–207, June 17–19, 2002.
8. National Institute of Standards and Technology (NIST). NIST statistical test suite. http://csrc.nist.gov/rng/rng2.html, Accessed January 23, 2007.
9. Nessus Project. Nessus vulnerability scanner. http://www.nessus.org/, Accessed January 23, 2007.
10. Oxid.it. Cain & Abel. http://www.oxid.it/, Accessed January 23, 2007.
11. Openwall Project. John the ripper password cracker. http://www.openwall.com/john/, Accessed January 23, 2007.
12. University of Oulo. PROTOS security testing of protocol implementations. http://www.ee.oulu.fi/research/ouspg/protos/index.html, Accessed January 23, 2007.

Cyber Defense Exercise: A Service Provider Model

Jeffrey A. Mattson

Software Engineering Institute, Carnegie Mellon University, 4500 5th Avenue, Pittsburgh, PA 15218
jmattson@cert.org

Abstract. Cyber Defense Exercises (CDX) continue to gain appreciation in the context of information security education. Primarily conducted in academic environments, the call for CDX is beginning to breach that boundary. Existing models are challenged by cost, agility, legality, and scope. This paper presents a model that addresses these challenges through a CDX service provider model.

Keywords: Cyber Defense Exercise, Training Information Assurance Professionals, Information Security Education.

1 Cyber Defense Exercise

Cyber Defense Exercises (CDX) are training events designed to educate participants in the field of information assurance and cyber security. The general concept requires a team to defend a computer network, including the hosts and devices that comprise the network. CDX has grown in popularity since 2001 when the United States Military Academy challenged her sister service academies to an information security competition. Many other universities have developed similar exercises, most often to directly support their information security curriculum. For the past two years, there has been an influx of schools engaging in these exercises through the National Collegiate Cyber Defense Competition [1]. The NCCDC has provided a format and structure that allows schools to compete locally and regionally toward the goal of reaching the annual national competition.

This popularity is driven by the significant impact that the hands-on, real-world training these events provide. The literature on cyber defense exercises consistently describes the enthusiasm of participants for the knowledge gained and lessons learned. An exercise of this sort serves as a natural capstone to a holistic information security education program.

The CERT[1] training program serves the professional community through a traditional educational model to build a knowledge foundation through lecture and demonstration, followed by confidence-building labs and exercises. In this "hear, see, do" structure, students gain not only knowledge, but experience as well.

---

[1] CERT is the Networked Systems Survivability program at Carnegie Mellon University's Software Engineering Institute. One of its missions focuses on the development and education of best practices for Information Assurance.

Please use the following format when citing this chapter:

Mattson, J., 2007, in IFIP International Federation for Information Processing, Volume 237, Fifth World Conference on Information Security Education, eds. Futcher, L., Dodge, R., (Boston: Springer), pp. 81–86.

1.1   Academic Boundary

The Cyber Defense Exercise Workshop, sponsored by the National Science Foundation in 2004, recommended the CDX stay confined for a time to the university setting [2]. The CDX process could better mature and incorporate into the information security discipline if its focus was initially on the academic exercise. It is clear, however, that some outside of academia are already interested in the training benefits a CDX can provide. All of the Armed Forces branches, as well as the Department of Defense as a whole, are looking for ways to validate the effectiveness of their Information Assurance professionals. The DoD 8570 directive requires personnel in information assurance positions are certified at an appropriate knowledge level [3]. The CDX may be a vehicle by which those goals can be met.

Many other government agencies are following suit. As the government is now implementing legislated requirements for the strengthening of information security processes, they are looking for ways to enhance their training. The Federal Information Security Management Act formalizes a rigorous review of information security processes for all government departments [4]. Included in those processes are mechanisms for workforce education and training.

It is likely that industry will follow. The University of Texas in San Antonio's 2006 CDX networks were defined as typical small business networks as that was a likely future environment for most of the participants [5]. As students who have benefited from this exercise permeate business environments, they may likely bring with them this idea of CDX training.

1.2   Training for Professionals

One of the common complaints of exercise participants, in the case of an early USMA Service Academy CDX, was lack of preparedness in network systems administration. This is explainable as "...the Computer Science Accreditation Board does not emphasize network administration, but rather software creation. Thus, these cadets learned the same lessons that system administrator would also learn by experience "[6]. This reinforces the point that a CDX can provide some experience to those without it; very similar to "on-the-job-training". This experience helps students understand the knowledge they have acquired in more traditional academic settings. However, by regretting their lack of experience, students imply a desire to undertake the exercise with the requisite experience. Consider then the effect of a CDX on IA professionals, those with varying degrees of experience already in hand. The focus shifts from gaining knowledge to demonstrating knowledge. The exercise can serve primarily as a continuing education, skills validation or a team-building exercise, rather than grounds for knowledge synthesis.

2   CDX Features

The Cyber Defense Exercise Workgroup defined four types of CDX popularly implemented: the organized CDX competition, the continuous internal exercise, the regional capture-the-flag exercise, and the class-integrated exercise. Of these four, the first is the best candidate for the expansion from academia to industry. If the focus of the exercise shifts from learning to validation, integration with a specific curriculum is no longer necessary. The continuous internal exercise has a bit of a game feel to it, and lacks a discrete ending point and performance review. The capture-the-flag model also lacks the structure and organization to effectively evaluate a team on cyber defense. The organized CDX offers the key features necessary for an evaluation exercise.

2.1 Defense

The participants are focused on network defense only. The legality of computer attacks makes any offensive effort of an exercise questionable. Especially in a validation of cyber defense skills, there seems to be little need for the participants to employ any offensive tactics. This scenario uses third-party IA professionals to objectively test the defenses of each team. As such, participants are not evaluated on attacks, but only on defense.

2.2 Administration

Exercise participants can be completely responsible for the administration of their networks. Because the exercise duration can be well defined, and generally short, the students are generally able to administer the networks from setup to tear-down. This applies to most event structures: both where networks are preconfigured and provided and those where participants must build and design a network of their choice.

2.3 Isolation

It is imperative that a CDX is conducted on an isolated network. Unfortunately, for a validation exercise this usually means some loss of realism. It would be ideal to evaluate participants' skills on the very network they maintain; however, the risks associated are generally too high. Any exercise incident, whether malicious or not, could end up affecting real-world events, so separate, isolated networks are highly encouraged. The level of realism the "range" network provides stems from availability of the organization's resources. In many cases it seems possible to construct a reasonably similar training network.

2.4 Competition

In the academic setting, much of the participant motivation is generated through competition. While competition may have less influence in a corporate or government evaluation environment, it can still play a part. Organization's that are large enough may submit several different teams to a CDX, and such intramural competition may be leveraged to strengthen enthusiasm. The primary motivation, however, comes from the desire of the participant to demonstrate his skill-set to his employer. As managers work to maintain a skilled workforce, often in need of some reportable measure of certification or compliance, they may find value in CDX and request employees to validate or assess their skills.

3   CDX Enhancements

To support the CDX at a much wider scope than currently employed, the CDX model can be enhanced and streamlined. It is foreseeable that IT training and education companies may add the CDX capability to their suite of offerings. Such a move would provide a significant service to those desiring a CDX. The difficulty and hassle of occasionally setting up and coordinating an exercise would vanish for an organization that was focused on delivering CDX services. As commercial opportunity grows for the management of CDX, we anticipate streamlined governance and exercise management, reduced costs, and more effective communication.

3.1   Virtualization

Constructing a CDX environment based on virtualization provides a significant improvement in scalability, agility, and isolation. Commercial products that provide the ability to create and run virtual machines have matured considerably in recent years. This provides a simple means to maximize use of the physical resources on hand. Thus, the number of physical hosts necessary to produce the exercise network is easily four times fewer than virtual machines.

A virtual environment is also one that maximizes agility. The ability to change directions quickly to meet new needs is fostered by virtualization products, especially those with snapshot capabilities. With a collection of base virtual hard disks, it can become a push-button operation to add new machines to the network or to revert all machines back to a known starting state. Customers of a CDX could potentially build their exercise network topology by just selecting a few menu options.

Further, virtualization generally provides built-in network isolation. The entire exercise network, including Red Team hosts, can be separated from other networks. Access to the exercise network could be through a portal, allowing participants to enter the lab environment from anywhere with network connectivity. This portal can provide participants with a remote session on a virtual host attached to the virtual network. With only the remote session desktop image being allowed out of the exercise network, returning to the participant's computer, the threat of a malicious event breaching the wall of isolation is mitigated. This concept allows for the formation of virtual teams -- participants who are not physically co-located but can contribute to the same mission from anywhere around the world.

3.2   Cost Reduction

While virtualization can ease the cost burden of procurement and maintenance, centralization of CDX services can also mitigate personnel costs. The service provider can fulfill multiple roles in the exercise conduct, such as exercise setup and management, referee, or White Team, and even the Red Team role. While it could be easy enough to provide a third party Red Team with virtual hosts in attack position, it is also feasible for the exercise controller to have at his disposal a set of scripted, push-button attacks. At any rate, the service provider model can significantly free the educators or managers time for other work.

3.3   Communication and Feedback

With the ability to handle virtual teams that connect to the exercise network from dispersed locations, providing communication services becomes mandatory. The exercise entry portal can be equipped to allow for intra-team and white team communication. Bandwidth options could allow either video, voice, or text chats, so that the team could assemble in a virtual room. Further, the portal can provide a logging mechanism to capture event information during the exercise. Because the whole of the network resides in the service provider's domain, they can capture real-time logs of exercise events, to include Red Team actions. This translates into rapid information collation and a support for a timely after-action review. In the traditional CDX, it is not uncommon for the assessment to follow the exercise by several weeks. Shortening this delay should increase the impact of any lessons learned because they would be offered much closer to the action.

3.4   Uniformity

To be effective as an assessment device or measuring tool, a CDX needs to provide a certain amount of uniformity across instantiations. Not only is it important for competition that all teams are on a level playing field, but it is just as necessary, and perhaps more challenging, to provide a similar exercise scenario to different teams. Currently this is done by conducting simultaneous exercises so that attackers and referees can inject events into the scenario uniformly to all teams. Then the question remains of uniformity from year to year, or even event to event.

One way to address this is through a formally, but flexibly, scripting the scenario. Providing detailed objectives, and defining various levels of success, allows results from different exercises to be compared with a higher degree of confidence. To borrow from the military's vocabulary, each event expected during the scenario can be broken into Tasks, Conditions, and Standards that allows for fine-grained assessments.

3.5   Other considerations

There are several issues yet to work out in a CDX service provider model as described. The issue of network devices affects the streamlined nature of a completely virtualized environment. Any use of physical devices would impact the agility and scalability with which a provider can offer services. While having physical devices may be essential to some environments, there are several in which exercise objectives could still be met using virtual replacements.

Also, it would be necessary to provide some means of downloading software or importing non-standard tools into an isolated exercise network. Without access to the physical machines, participants would need to coordinate with the service providers for this capability.

4   Conclusion

The CERT Practices, Development, and Training team has focused on improving Information Assurance Training for many years. The training concept used is reflected in the slogan "Knowledge in Depth for Defense in Depth". The KD3 program builds on a traditional education foundation of instructor led classes with lecture, demonstration, and hands-on lab exercises. Following individual training, teams need be trained on both network assessment and cyber defense. Because this team training is increasingly sought after and difficult to reproduce, it is an excellent candidate for implementation under a CDX service provider model. To fulfill the growing call for this effective, exciting training, the future of CDX development should aim in this direction.

References

1. National Collegiate Cyber Defense Competition. *http://nationalccdc.org/history.html.*
2. Lance J. Hoffman, Tim Rosenberg, Ronald Dodge, and Daniel Ragsdale, "Exploring a National Cybersecurity Exercise for Universities," *IEEE Security & Privacy*, vol. 3, no. 5, September/October 2005, pp. 27-33.
3. U.S. Department of Defense Directive 8570, *Information Assurance Training, Certification, and Workforce Management*, August 15, 2004.
4. Federal Information Security Management Act (P.L. 107-347, Title III), December 2002.
5. Art Conklin, "Cyber Defense Competitions and Information Security Education: An Active Learning Solution for a Capstone Course", in *Proceedings of the 39th Hawaii International Conference on System Sciences*, 2006.
6. Donald Welch, Daniel Ragsdale, and Wayne Schepens, "Training for Information Assurance", *IEEE Computer*, vol. 35, no. 4, March 2002, pp. 30-37.

Information Security Specialist Training for the Banking Sphere

Andrey P.Kurilo, Natalia G.Miloslavskaya and Alexander I.Tolstoy

[1] The Central Bank of Russia,
[2] Moscow Engineering Physics Institute (State University), Moscow, Russia
+7 495 324-9735, ait@mephi.edu, tolstoy@mephi.ru

Abstract. On the basis of analysis of the Standard of the Central Bank of Russia "Ensuring Information Security for Organizations of Banking system of the Russian Federation. Basic principles." there have been defined the qualification requirements for the specialists with higher education in the field of information security who could be claimed for work in the banking sphere.

Keywords: information security, expert training, banking sphere, Russia

1 Introduction

Banking institutions are one of the most sensitive objects for which information security (IS) maintenance requirements are very real. Damage from breaking the security of banking information (confidentiality, integrity, and availability) could have a wide range of consequences ranging from financial loss of individuals to financial crisis of an individual state.

The banking system of the Russian Federation is formed by the Central Bank of Russia, different credit organizations (for e.g., the Savings Bank, the Vneshtorgbank, the Vnesheconombank, regional banks etc.), and representative and branch offices of foreign banks. These organizations solve different business problems and have different structures (for e.g., have or have not regional branches).

The joining factor for different banking objects is the banking information and banking information technologies. The peculiarities of the banking information and technologies allow us to allocate banking organizations into a separate groups of information objects that require separate approaches to IS. These approaches apply to the whole object and its separate systems (like automated banking payment systems, information banking systems, telecommunication banking systems). Compounding the variability in requirements, IS employees require specialized training in the field of IS.

Training of specialists with higher education in the field of IS is carried out by over 100 Russian universities. Analysis of the experience collected within training of IS specialists in one of the leading Russian universities – the Moscow Engineering Physiscs Institute (State University), which has the Information Security of Banking Systems Department at the Information Security Faculty – allow forming the basic requirements to the level of preparation of specialists for the banking sphere.

Please use the following format when citing this chapter:

Kurilo, A., Miloslavskaya, N., Tolstoy, A., 2007, in IFIP International Federation for Information Processing, Volume 237, Fifth World Conference on Information Security Education, eds. Futcher, L., Dodge, R., (Boston: Springer), pp. 87–93.

To form such kind of requirements it is expedient to examine the types and tasks of professional activities of the university graduates and to formulate their qualification characteristics. The following sections formulate the qualification characteristics of IS specialists for banking institutions.

2   Defining Qualification Characteristics

The basic qualification characteristics of a specialist with higher education are formulated on the basis of his/her special (professional) competences. Special qualitites of a graduate are his/her abilities to solve definite problems and carry out specific work within his/her line.

Thus formulating the qualification characteristics is possible only when considering separate typical objects where IS tasks are carried out with specialists in the IS field. Such kind of qualification characteristics could be formulated on the basis of expert estimations of either leading IS specialists or definite organizations. Unfortunately the second approach cannot be easily implemented in practice because of lack of distinct system which would allow joining forces of separate typical organizations for working out concrete qualification requirements.

It is necessary to note that this drawback concerning banking instituations of Russia has been overcome with adopting the Standard of the Central Bank of Russia (SCBR) "Ensuring Information Security in Organizations of Banking System of the Russian Federation. Basic principles." in 2006 [1]. There is enough information within the Standard to formulate the qualification requirements for specialists, ensuring functioning of the banking information protection systems.

3   Initial data for formulating the qualification characteristics

It is possible to formulate qualification characteristics on the basis of:
- topics worked out by students within a specific banking organization during their practice and preparation of graduate qualification paper (diploma project);
- functions of IS specialists working within concrete banking objects.

Under the first qualification characteristic, the Russian universities allow up to one year for practicing and preparation of the graduate qualification paper for training IS specialists. For example, the MEPhI students have their 10th and 11th semesters for that which lasts for 1 year. Experience of graduating higher education specialists collected since 1995 allow grouping practice and diploma project topics in the following way:
- development of information protection technologies;
- design of information protection means;
- administering separate IS technologies;
- administering IS subsystems;
- IS subsystem design for a concrete automated system;

- IS management system design of an object as a whole.

It is worth noting that for banking information objects the most typical or the topics that deal with administering separate information technologies and IS technologies, design and administering IS subsystems of concrete automated systems and design of IS management systems for an object as a whole.

Developing of specialized information protection means for banking information objects is not actual.

Considering the second qualification characteristic, to define functions of IS specialists working within banking objects it is necessary to define a place of IS at those objects, role of IS service and line of activities of such specialists. Such information could be obtained upon analysis of the SCBR. Before analyzing the document, it is expedient to characterize that Standard in general.

4 General Characteristic of the SCBR "Ensuring Information Security for Organizations of the Banking system of the Russian Federation. Basic principles."

The SCBR consists of three main parts:

1. Forming the goals of ensuring IS of banking organizations in the Russian Federation (RF) (is based upon defining initial conceptual scheme (paradigm) of IS, basic principles of IS, model of threats and IS violators and forming IS policy of an organization).

2. Implementation of the goals of ensuring IS of an organization. This part of the SCBR defines the role of IS management processes in an organization.

3. Control of progress in reaching IS goals of an organization is based upon checks and evaluation of organization's IS (monitoring and audit) and defining maturity of organization's IS management processes (defining maturity model).

When developing the SCBR a large number of international (14) and Russian (11) standards and normative documents were used. Moreover, a certain number of the Russian standards have foreign prototypes. Such as "ISO/IEC IS 27001-2005 Information technology. Security techniques. Information security management systems. Requirements" and "ISO/IEC IS 27002-2007 Information Technology. Code of practice for information security management."

The structure of the SCBR is the following:

- Scope of implemetation.
- Normative links.
- Terms and definitions.
- Notations and abbreviations.
- Initial conceptual scheme (paradigm) of ensuring IS of banking organizations in the RF.
- Basic principles of ensuring IS of banking organizations in the RF.
- Threat model and IS violator model of banking organizations in the RF.
- IS policy of banking organizations in the RF.
- IS management system of banking organizations in the RF.

- Check and evaluation of IS of banking organizations in the RF.
- Model of maturity of IS management processes of banking organizations in the RF.
- Standard's line of development.

Analysis of these sections of the SCBR allow us to get initial information for formulating qualification characteristics of IS specialists for banking organizations.

5   The Role of IS at the Object

The Standard defines the role of IS at the banking object as (section 5.2 of the Standard): *IS processes are a type of supplementary processes implementing support (ensuring) for the processes of the main activities of the organization for it to be able to reach the maximum result possible. It is also defined that organization's activities is carried out through 3 groups of high level processes: main processes (main business processes), supplementary processes (processes maintaining specific tasks) and organization management processes.*

Thus all the processes related to ensuring IS at an information object should add to the main business of the organization. As a result, when training IS specialists peculiarities of protection objects should be taken into consideration and that should be reflected at the qualification characteristics.

IS goal at an object is to build an optimal protection system which would ensure the required level of protection for information resources. That level is defined on the basis of analysis of IS risks which should be adjusted with the main sphere (business) of an organization (section 5.1 of the Standard).

Along with that, one has to note that any coordinated activity of an organization is forming risks whose essence is natural vagueness of the future. This is objective reality and those risks could be lowered only to the level of vagueness of subjects characterizing the nature of business. The remaining part of the risk defined by the factors of the environment of organization's processes for which organization cannot influence at all, should be accepted. In this case ensuring IS at an object should lower risks to a certain level.

6   IS Service Role at an Object

To specify the role of IS service in an organization it is necessary to define subjects that could interact with each other in situations when IS risks could appear. The standard defines the following subjects for that: owner of information assets of the organization and violator trying to influence those assets.

Information assets of the Russian banking system are defined by the Standard as different types of banking information (payment, financial and analytical, official, management, etc.) at all phases of its lifecycle (generation, processing, storage, transfer, termination).

Role of the IS service in an organization is defined by the tasks which are carried out within the conditions of opposition of the owner and violator for the control over information assets.

Ensuring IS at an object is the process that should be efficiently managed. The main role of IS service if defined by the organization's IS strategy which lies in *deployment, exploitation and perfection of the IS management system (ISMS)* (section 5.17 of the Standard).

IS management is a part of the overall corporate organization's management which is oriented for reaching organization's goals through ensuring protection of its information resources. ISMS of organizations is a part of the overall management system based on the business risk approach whose goal is to create, implement, operate, monitor, analyze, support and rise IS of an organization (ISO/IEC IS 27001).

7   IS Specialist Line of Activity

Upon defining the main lines of activities of IS specialists in a banking organization it is necessary to take the following quotations from the SCBR into consideration:

- *The most correct and efficient way of minimizing risks of IS breach for an owner is to develop an IS policy upon en exact forecast which is also based on analysis and evaluation of IS risks, and implement, operate and perfect the ISMS of an organization* (section 5.8 of the Standard). *Such kind of forecast could and should be built upon the experience of the leading specialist of the banking system and in accordance with international experience in the field* (section. 5.10 of the Standard).

- *IS policy of banking organization of the RF is built upon principles of ensuring IS of banking organizations of the RF, models of threats and violators, identification of assets being subject to protection, risk evaluation taking into account peculiarities of business and technologies and interest of a specific owner* (section 5.9 of the Standard).

- *Following IS policy is also an element of corporate ethics. That is why the level of IS within an organization is seriously influenced by team relations and also by team and owner (or management representing owner's interest) relations. Thus such kind of relations should be managed* (section 5.11 of the Standard).

- *Ensuring IS of an organization includes implementation and support of the process of perception of IS and IS management* (section 5.16 of the Standard). Perception of IS ensures the basis for ISMS's functioning. Here efficiency means relation between the achieved result and the spent resources.

- *To implement tasks of deployment and operation of the ISMS of an organization it is recommended to have IS service as part of the stuff* (section 9.7.1 of the Standard).

- To administer IS subsystems in cenrain automated banking systems the Standard assumes availability of specialists acting as IS administrators (section 8.2.9.5 of the Standard) and formulates basic requirements for such specialists.

Taking all this into consideration and the place and role of the object's IS service, it is possible to formulate the basic line of activities and qualification characteristics of an IS specialist working in banking organizations.

8   Basic Lines of Activities and Qualification Characteristics

The basic lines of activities of IS specialists in banking organizations are defined by their professional activity. Taking into consideration the requirements of the Standard and the topics of the graduate qualification papers allows to define the main types of professional activity:

- technological (ensuring functioning of the main IS technologies);
- organizational-technological (ensuring functioning of ISMS).

Qualification requirements are defined by the types of tasks carried out by the specialists and requirements for the level of knowledge and skills. There are the following tasks solved (special competence):

- formation of goals of ensuring IS at the object on the basis of identification of object's assets, risk analysis, evaluation of IS risks, definition of basic principles of ensuring IS and formulation of object's IS policy.
- implementation of goals for ensuring IS at the object on the basis of deployment, operation and perfection of ISMS.
- control over achievement, if IS at the object goals on the basis of the processes of monitoring, conducting self-evaluation of level of object's IS and definition of level of maturity of object's IS management.

Further, IS specialists should –

know:

- normative basics, related to ensuring IS;
- principles of ensuring IS;
- methods of IS risk analysis;
- basic methods of IS management;

be able to:

- define model of threats and model of IS violators;
- develop an IS policy;
- conduct IS risk analysis at the object;
- develop, deploy, operate, perfect ISMS;
- administer IS subsystems of certain information technologies and automated systems;

have an idea of:

- methods of building object management systems;
- methods of system monitoring and audit;
- peculiarities of psychology and ethics of team relations.

An example collection of activities that should be carried out by an IS specialist working in an IS service of a banking organization is (section 9.7.1 of the Standard):

- manage all the plans of ensuring organization's IS;
- develop and propose modifications to the IS policy;

- modify existing and adopt new normative and methodical documents for ensuring organization's IS;
- choose means of management and ensuring IS of an organization;
- control users and first of all users who have maximum privileges;
- control activity related to access and use of anti-virus tools and other means of IS;
- monitor events related to IS;
- investigate events related to violations of IS and if needed propose application of sanctions against people, who have done unlawful activity, for example, infringed requirements of instructions, manuals, etc. for organization's IS;
- participate in activities for recovery of operational capacity of automated systems right after faults and accidents;
- create, support and perfect ISMS of the organization.

9 Conclusion

On the basis of analysis of the Standard of the Central Bank of Russia "Ensuring Information Security for Organizations of Banking system of the Russian Federation. Basic principles." the qualification requirements for specialists with higher education in the field of IS have been defined. These qualifications must be met prior to working in the banking sphere. These qualification requirements have universality and do not depend upon national peculiarities of banking systems. Additionally, the process of formulation of qualification requirements could be used for definition of qualification requirements for specialists dealing with other typical objects. Higher education institutes can use the defined qualification requirements for specific training plans and contents of training.

References

1. The Standard of the Central Bank of Russia "Ensuring Information Security for Organizations of Banking system of the Russian Federation. Basic principles." STO BR IBBS-1.0-2006.

Learning Security through Computer Games: Studying user behavior in a real-world situation

Kjell Näckros

[1] The Department of Computer and Systems Sciences, Stockholm University and
Royal Institute of Technology, Sweden
kjellna@dsv.su.se

Abstract. This paper discusses how learning material in the form of computer games in the area of ICT security affect ICT security usage. The findings from a conducted user-study show that computer games can be efficient learning environments when using security tools in terms of accessibility, safety, and speed. By replicating an earlier usability study, in which the participants utilised security tools to send and receive encrypted emails, the practical consequences of learning via a Game-Based Instruction were evaluated; the findings show that none of the participants who were given the chosen computer game as an instruction before the actual assignment did make any serious error when applying their security knowledge in contrast to the participants who did not receive any instruction in forehand. They also finished the assignment faster than the corresponding participants. To be able to evaluate the "practical knowledge" acquired, a model for Vital Security Functions was created that allows for comparison of security usage between high-level security applications.

Keywords: ICT Security, Education, Game-Based Instruction, GBI, Computer Games, Game-Based Learning, GBL, Knowledge, Vital Security Functions, VSF, Linear instruction, Nonlinear instruction, Learning preferences

1 Introduction

Current learning materials in ICT security have a tendency to fit certain individuals better than others. This in turn increases the feeling of insecurity for those who do not understand and therefore also increase the ICT vulnerabilities in the systems they are using. Therefore it is important to find alternative and/or complementary learning materials that will stimulate learning/understanding of ICT security issues also for these individuals, in order to strengthen the viability of the system as a whole. Within ICT security, Yngström [1] p.160 has discussed that "... educators will have to pay attention to developing new educational tools, which will stimulate and support various learning preferences ..." Fred Cohen's work within scenario-based training [2] resulted in the development of security games, however, in the opinion of this author, these games did not have the nonlinear dimension and were not developed with

Please use the following format when citing this chapter:

Näckros, K., 2007, in IFIP International Federation for Information Processing, Volume 237, Fifth World Conference on Information Security Education, eds. Futcher, L., Dodge, R., (Boston: Springer), pp. 95–103.

learning preferences in mind. Is it possible that individuals having difficulties with current linear learning materials will increase their knowledge and comprehension in the area of ICT security, if a nonlinear computer game is used?

But, to develop a Game-Based Instruction (GBI) is expensive. Because it often requires more people with different types of expertise involved throughout the development process as compared to developing a conventional linear instruction. Furthermore, findings from a similar studies [3], [4], [5], investigating the theoretical knowledge acquired via GBI, indicated that the learning process itself takes more time using a GBI as compared to a linear instruction.

When evaluating an instruction within ICT security it is necessary to consider what the learners actually learn; there is a need to investigate not only the theoretical knowledge acquired but also the applicability of the acquired knowledge, i.e. how the learners apply their theoretical knowledge in real-world situations.

If the usage of computer games as instruction leads to odd or distinguished risky behaviour when applying ICT security functions in real-world situations there is a reason not to favour further usage. While if the usage indicates a distinguished "sound" ICT security behaviour e.g. conducting few "dangerous" mistakes, this type of instruction may be considered despite the overhead cost generated by the development.

To possess theoretical ICT security knowledge does not necessarily imply a better or more affordable usage of ICT security tools in practise. In fact, the opposite is possible. It is possible that theoretical information distracts or confuses many users during usage; the security application's user interface seldom maps the terminology or the principles upon which the security application is based. Different applications use different kinds of analogies to aid the user in controlling the security functions. A user with only theoretical knowledge may, for example, search for functions hidden to the normal user; the application may (or may not) handle the functions automatically, i.e. transparently to the user in favour for an easily understood working environment. The user may, for example, hesitate pushing that particular button, required by the situation, because s/he does not know the exact consequences of the action, and may lose a sense of control.

During a previous conducted study, evaluating the theoretical security knowledge acquired through GBI [3] certain user behaviours among the participants were noticed. Based on these user behaviours it may be reasonable to assume that a user with only theoretical knowledge about ICT security will tend to:

- hesitate to execute functions, because lack of information about the function in conjunction with knowledge about possible consequences, and therefore
- spend time trying to map the application's terminology with their own knowledge.
- check and recheck the result of their actions instead of take a chance.

Consequently, it may also be reasonable to assume that a user without theoretical knowledge will:

- compare the usage with other applications, instead of trying to understand the security functions.
- learn through trial and error, and because of this
- make dangerous errors

- obtain a false sense of security; the application responds as expected e.g. no alert window, telling there is something wrong or a message box telling everything is ok.

These assumptions have guided the design of the study.

This paper presents parts of the findings from research on computer games' general affect on learning outcome within ICT security (ibid.), focusing on the question; how learning material in the form of computer games in the area of ICT security affect ICT security *usage*?

2 Method

This study replicates parts of an earlier study, in which Whitten and Tygar [6] investigated 12 individuals' ability to learn and use the public key encryption tool PGP 5 from Network Associates concerning the usability aspect.

The practical consequences of using an educational computer game, the Paradise GBI [3], [5], were investigated as follows:

- User-study on a real-world assignment using an earlier study [6] as a model.
- Development of a model – for evaluating the applicability of ICT security knowledge – so called, VSF-model within PKI.
- Two different analyses of the collected data according to the VSF- model (this paper will only present the first analysis.)

The applicability of the knowledge acquired through the GBI prototype was investigated and evaluated by reconstructing parts of an earlier study [6] where the participants had to perform a real-world ICT security assignment. The results from the two studies were compared and discussed.

A framework for evaluating and comparing Vital Security Functions (VSF-model) within a high-level security tool was created and used to evaluate the results. Time was a vital factor for comparing each participant's solution to the assignment. Other collected data included age, gender, interests, and preferable learning style. During the actual real-world ICT security assignment screen recordings and observations were collected.

The analysis investigated if learners who receive learning material in the form of a computer game (the Paradise GBI) will make fewer mistakes in a real-world ICT security assignment in PKI than those who receive none. "Fewer mistakes" was put in contrast to the results from the Whitten and Tygar study in which the participants did not have previous theoretical knowledge about PKI. The analysis compares the number of dangerous errors and time to fulfil the assignment by using data from VSF State table (see section 3.2). Since, in the Whitten and Tygar study "... only one third of them were able to use PGP to correctly sign and encrypt an email message when given 90 minutes in which to do so. Furthermore, one quarter of them accidentally exposed the secret they were meant to protect in the process, by sending it in email they thought they had encrypted but had not" (ibid. p.21) it was interesting to compare how the participants in this Study differed in managing a similar assignment from the participants in the Whitten and Tygar study. The independent variable would thus be the Paradise GBI, which the participants in this Study used prior to the assignment, and the participants in the Whitten and Tygar study did not.

2.1 Methodological considerations

When reconstructing a study it is almost impossible to meet exactly the same conditions on different occasions, it is simply difficult to identify what parameters caused any possible differences between the outcomes of the studies.

- **Time** – The Whitten and Tygar study was conducted in 1998 and the second study in this thesis in 2003; it is a time difference of five years. In five years, a lot has happened within ICT and ICT usage that may influence the findings of the latter study.
- **Place** – The Whitten and Tygar study was conducted at Carnegie Mellon University, Pennsylvania, USA and this study was conducted at Stockholm University, Sweden.
- **Culture** – It is possible that the test users' cultural differences may influence the findings.
- **Purpose of the study** – The Whitten and Tygar study investigated the usability of a particular public key encryption application using two different methods. This Study investigated the applicability of the test users' pre-knowledge on a particular public key encryption application.
- **Participant's fee** – In the Whitten and Tygar study, the researchers offered $20 in cash, whereas in the latter study the participants did not receive any money.

Although, the purpose for investigation differs between the two studies, it is still possible to use the data collected to make interesting and possible comparable statements about the learning situation itself.

2.2 Defining a model

To be able to analyse and compare collected data from a security functionality perspective, there was a need to identify the Vital Security Functions (VSF) necessary to achieve secure communication of information according public key encryption concepts realised in PGP 5.

By using VSF it is possible to neglect the user interface and the different analogies that differentiate the high-level security applications and evaluate according to the purpose of the application instead. Therefore, data within this model ought to be comparable for other high-level PKI applications as well.

The first step was to identify all PKI related choices the participant was faced with at different states when achieving the assignment. During this process, a VSF Use Case diagram, see Figure 1, was sketched.

In the second step, the relations between states were identified and a VSF State diagram was created. The VSF State diagram was needed to identify the necessary order between states.

When the VSF states and the necessary order between the VSF states were identified a table for the VSFs was created in Table 1. The VSF State table shows the different VSF states, the necessary order between the states and the time when the participant reached a certain state.

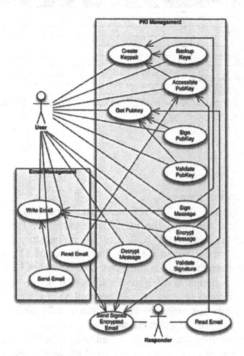

Fig. 1. Simplified VSF Use case diagram

The VSF State table is suitable when comparing and analysing numerical data, investigating for example the number of individuals that reached state "I" (accomplishing the assignment), or the average "time" for a group of individuals reaching a certain state. VSF State table is sufficient to answer if learners who receive learning material as the Paradise GBI will conduct fewer mistakes in a real-world ICT security assignment in PKI than those who receive none and is used in the analysis.

The number of participants successfully reaching state "I" in Table 1 was compared between the Whitten and Tygar study and this Study. The average of time to reach state "I" was also calculated and compared.

The number of conducted dangerous errors at the group of participants that did not finish the assignment was compared between the Whitten and Tygar study and this Study. A dangerous error during PKI usage is some act violating a basic concept of PKI e.g. making the private key publicly available to unauthorised individuals, or sending a secret message without suitable encryption applied to it.

Table 1. VSF State table

Activity ID	State	Preceding activities	Time to reach State (min) Participant x x
A	Message	-	
B	Keypair	-	
C	Accessible Public Key	B	
D	Receivers Public Key	-	
E	Validated Public Key	D	
F	Encrypted Message	A,D	
G	Signed Message	A,B	
H	Signed Encrypted Message	A,B,D	
I	Sent Sign./Encr. Message	A,H,C	

In the table it is also possible to see who, when and at what VSF State a participant failed the assignment.

3   Result

The findings from analysis showed:

- **Accessibility.** The Paradise GBI increased the participant's accessibility to the encryption software. The participants using the Paradise GBI before conducting the real-world ICT security assignment, all completed the security assignment within the time limit (12 out of 12), in contrast to the participants from the Whitten and Tyger study (5 out of 12 participants).
- **Safety.** The participants using the Paradise GBI before conducting the real-world ICT security assignment did not violate any basic PKI concept i.e. made no dangerous error. In the Whitten and Tygar study, 3 out of 12 participant exposed the secret message.
- **Speed.** The participants using the Paradise GBI before conducting the real-world ICT security assignment completed the assignment in average faster than the participants from the Whitten and Tygar study, and did so without being prompted from the test-monitor as in the Whitten and Tygar study.

The analysis compares data from two different studies, the Whitten and Tygar study (1998) and this Study. Subjected to analysis are mainly a) the number of dangerous errors and b) time to fulfil the assignment, using data from VSF State table.

The participants' results are presented in Table 2. The twelve participants (P) in the upper area are from the Whitten and Tygar study (a) and the twelve participants in the lower area are the results from this Study (b).

Since the Whitten and Tygar study had a different research focus, each participant's transcript from that study had to be re-transcribed into the new VSF-model format and some data could not be transformed into the new format. These values are intentionally left out in the table; the activity "C" and "I", which are needed to complete the assignment are, however, included. If a value is missing at activity "C" or "I", it means that the participant failed to complete the assignment.

In the table it is also possible to see who, when and at what VSF State a participant failed the assignment.

In the Whitten and Tygar study only five participants out of twelve succeeded to fulfil the real-world ICT security assignment within the time limit of 90 minutes, "and they did so only after they had received fairly explicit email prompting from the test monitor posing as the team members" (ibid. p.18).

Table 2. Results (VSF State table); a) Whitten and Tygar study, b) current study

Activity	State	Preceding activities	P1-a	P2-a	P3-a	P4-a	P5-a	P6-a	P7-a	P8-a	P9-a	P10-a	P11-a	P12-a
A	Message	-	5			5	5	5			5		5	25
B	Keypair	-	15	25	5	-		15	25	5	-	15	-	10
C	Accessible Public Key	B	35	60	90			30	55			60		15
D	Receivers Public Key	-	85		55			35		45		35		20
E	Validated Public Key	D					40							
F	Encrypted Message	A,D												
G	Signed Message	A,B												
H	Signed Encrypted Message	A,B,D												
I	Sent Sign./Encr. Message	A,H,C			85			45		50		40		45

Activity	State	Preceding activities	P1-b	P2-b	P3-b	P4-b	P5-b	P6-b	P7-b	P8-b	P9-b	P10-b	P11-b	P12-b
A	Message	-	17	39	5	18	23	3	10	27	16	10	4	32
B	Keypair	-	24	16	13	9	8	40	43	7	12	6	13	11
C	Accessible Public Key	B	63	57	38	17	30	51	43	7	12	39	13	18
D	Receivers Public Key	-	54	25	17	45	21	17	20	42	23	21	15	27
E	Validated Public Key	D	58	51							26			
F	Encrypted Message	A,D	59											
G	Signed Message	A,B	62											
H	Signed Encrypted Message	A,B,D		52	19	47	26	42	46	43	36	30	19	35
I	Sent Sign./Encr. Message	A,H,C	64	52	19	47	30	42	46	43	39	30	19	35

In Table 2 it is shown that, of the participants that did not use the Paradise GBI before conducting the security assignment (the participants from the Whitten and Tygar study):

- 8 out of 12 participants had reached a VSF within 5 min.
- 4 out of 12 participants failed to fulfil the assignment because of violating a basic PKI concept i.e. exploiting a secret message or exploiting a private key.
- 1 out of 12 participants validated the authenticity of the receiver's public key.
- 5 out of 12 participants finished all the necessary VSFs.
- Average time for finishing the security assignment: 58 min. (5 participants).

In Table 2 is also shown that, of the participants that used the Paradise GBI before conducting the security assignment (the participants from this Study):

- 12 out of 12 participants finished all the necessary VSFs to complete the security assignment.
- 3 out of 12 participants validated the authenticity of the receiver's public key.
- Average time for finishing the security assignment: 42 min. (12 participants).

Generally, it seems that the Paradise GBI has had a positive effect on the participants' usage of the PGP encryption software.

Despite a general understanding of PKI, acquired through the Paradise GBI, only 3 out of 12 participants verified the authenticity of the receiver's public key/certificate. Most of the participants were satisfied with what appears to be the receiver's name associated with the key, something anyone may associate with whatever name of choice. Apparently, future GBIs in PKI have to stress the importance of validating keys/certificates.

Since the PGP software has a built-in function that enables both encrypting and signing of data simultaneously, it is difficult to verify if the participants actually were aware of the distinction in practice, 11 out of 12 participants chose to use this multi-function instead of encrypting and signing separately.

4 Discussions and further research

GBI seems to have an overall positive effect on ICT security usage. In the study presented all the participants accomplished the real-world PKI assignment within the time-limit without making any dangerous error i.e. all participants in the real-world assignment managed to send and sign asymmetric encrypted data to the intended receivers in a successful way.

It was noteworthy that the participants used eleven different solutions to solve the assignment. Maybe not all participants would have completed the ICT security assignment if the possibilities to approach the assignment, were limited. It would be interesting to investigate the consequences of the ability to have the freedom of choice to conduct the assignment; what if the choices were limited. Does the freedom of choice influence the ICT security understanding and/or influence the number of dangerous errors?

During the assignment certain behaviours were also observed among the participants that could be an expression of a more "secure" and a more "insecure" behaviour, which would be interesting to study further.

Are GBI motivated to develop particularly for the area of ICT security? Because of the complex dynamic multidimensional nature of modern ICT security, it is this researcher's opinion that there is a need to be open-minded in the search for new educational means; nonlinear instructions like GBIs are definitely an interesting complement to conventional instruction in the effort to understand ICT security. GBIs are usually more expensive to develop but by using GBI frameworks, which combine design of computer games and design of instructional teaching methods, the development process can be less complex and less expensive leading to a higher amount of quality as a result which may also be evaluated and improved.

GBI is not a substitute for conventional instruction but an optional complement.

References

[1] Yngström, L. (1996) *A systemic-holistic approach to academic programmes in IT security.* Ph.d. thesis: Report series no. 96-021, issn 1101-8526, isrn su-kth/dsv/r–96/21–se, Stockholm University (SU) / Royal Institute of Technology (KTH).

[2] Cohen, F. (1998), "Fred Cohen and associates", http://all.net, (Accessed 2 Nov 2006)

[3] Näckros, K. (2002), Game-based learning within it security education. In H. Armstrong and L. Yngström, editors, Wise2: Proceedings for the IFIP TC11 WG11.8 Second World Conference on Information Security Education, pages 243–260, Perth, Australia, 2001.

School of Computer and Information Science, Edith Cowan University, Perth, Western Australia.

[4] Näckros, K. and Yngström L. (2004), Applied holistic approach for security awareness and training. In ISSA2004: Proceedings for the fourth annual conference ISSA in IT Security, Johannesburg, South Africa, 2004.

[5] Näckros, K. (2005). *Visualising Security through Computer Games: Investigating Game-Based Instruction inICT Security: an Experimental Approach*. Ph.d. thesis: Report series no. 05-014, isbn 91-7155-077-1, issn 1101-8526, isrn su-kth/dsv/r–05/14–se, Stockholm University (SU) / Royal Institute of Technology (KTH).

[6] Whitten, A. and J. D. Tygar (1998), Usability of security: a case study. Technical Report CMU-CS-98-155, Carnegie Mellon University, Pennsylvania, USA.

Forensic Computing Training, Certification and Accreditation: An Australian Overview

Matthew Simon, Jill Slay

Centre of Excellence in Defence and Industry Systems Capability (CEDISC),
Defence and Systems Institute, University of South Australia,
Mawson Lakes Campus, Mawson Lakes,
SA5095, AUSTRALIA
{matthew.simon, jill.slay}@unisa.edu.au

Abstract. Training, certification and accreditation are concepts that are used in almost all aspects of professional life. This paper reviews current initiatives in Forensic Computing training and certification in Australia and the effect of this on National Accreditation processes.

Keywords: Forensic Computing; Training; Certification; Education.

1   Introduction

Training, certification and accreditation are concepts that are used in almost all aspects of professional life. The level of training required for most jobs can vary substantially from zero, to on the job training, to a degree qualification. Driving a forklift in South Australia requires the operator to hold a forklift licence. To get a licence, the applicant must be "*assessed by a registered assessor as being competent to operate the equipment in accordance with the competency standards in the national loadshifting guidelines*" [1]. In this case, the licence certifies that the holder can operate a forklift to an acceptable standard. Similarly, a medical doctor may need to study for up to seven years, and then do an internship before getting a medical licence. Certification shows that the certified entity meets specific competencies or criteria [2] . It not only allows people to make judgements based on that certification, but also provides a constant minimum standard.

Within the field of forensic computing there is currently a problem with both training and certification of practitioners, and the accreditation of laboratories. This is because there is no unified list of standards and competencies within the domain [3]. The domain is not without some certifications and accreditations, for example, ISO 17025 can be applied to accredit any general laboratory and ASCLD-LAB is a special purpose forensic laboratory accreditation. These accreditations have had a positive impact on the direction of the development of the forensic computing field. Beckett [2] references prominent authors in the field of forensic computing who have commented on the "*chaotic*" manner in which the field has developed in the ten years previous,

Please use the following format when citing this chapter:

Simon, M., Slay, J., 2007, in IFIP International Federation for Information Processing, Volume 237, Fifth World Conference on Information Security Education, eds. Futcher, L., Dodge, R., (Boston: Springer), pp. 105–112.

attributing this mainly to a lack of formal and standardised certification. This development of the field has prevented forensic computing from being regarded as a mature forensic science.

2   Background

Forensic computing can be described as the investigation into criminal or unethical activities which may have left digital evidence (Mohay 2005). Although this definition appears simplistic, it specifies the existence of digital evidence, which is the very core of 'computing' in the term forensic computing. The forensic aspect of forensic computing is equally important and - in a modern sense,- literally describes "any professional practice that provides scientific knowledge to the trier of fact" [2] . Beckett [2] lists a number of disciplines which have common forensic applications such as Biology, Firearms -Ballistics and Handwriting. Patel and Ó Ciardhuáin [4] describe the purpose of forensic computing as "...to collect tangible evidence showing that some unacceptable action has been carried out using methods which are themselves acceptable". Defining acceptable methods for use within forensic computing is problematic due to a lack of standardised certification, accreditation and training within the field.

The forensic practices and processes used to recover and evaluate evidence during an investigation are of the utmost importance as it is likely they will be scrutinised when presented in court. Having a sound investigation technique is crucial for evidence admissibility and credibility of the investigators. The issue currently facing forensic computing is a lack of consistent standards and competencies to unify the field as a solid science [2]. Compared with other domains of forensic science - some of which are over 100 years old - forensic computing is relatively young and is still developing. These other fields have had time to mature and as such have developed formal methodologies, standards and competencies.

It is generally accepted that a professional career in most domains is based on a specific body of knowledge, training and accreditation. However, this does not appear to be the case in forensic computing. Valli (cited in [2]) points out that information technology commonly relies on certification rather than formal tertiary qualifications as a means of industry credentials. Beckett [2] further explains by arguing that information technology is the only industry that relies so heavily on such certifications. He goes on to list examples of trade careers which all require a set number of years as an apprentice and formal studies before being fully qualified.

Within Australian Commonwealth law there is no formal specification of what constitutes an expert witness. It is unclear whether an expert must have relevant formal qualifications or if experience alone is enough [5]. A person who has completed a vendor-based course —an EnCase user course for example- may claim to be an expert witness simply because they can use and understand output from the specific tool. Beckett [2] however, contends that an expert should have greater knowledge than how to use a single tool as a greater understanding of the material being examined is required. Meyers & Rogers [3] report that no evidence has yet been made inadmissible as a direct result of not knowing the internal workings of the software, but this does not mean that it is not a future possibility. McDougall [6] lists guidelines specified by the New South Wales Supreme Court for allowing expert testimony:

1. it must be agreed or demonstrated that there is a field of "specialised knowledge";
2. there must be an identified aspect of that field in which the witness demonstrates that by reason of specified training, study or experience, the witness has become an expert;
3. the opinion proffered must be "wholly or substantially based on the witness's expert knowledge";
4. so far as the opinion is based on facts "observed" by the expert, they must be identified and admissibly proved by the expert;
5. so far as the opinion is based on "assumed" or "accepted" facts, they must be identified and proved in some other way;
6. it must be established that the facts on which the opinion is based form a proper foundation for it; and the expert's evidence must explain how the field of "specialised knowledge" in which the witness is expert, and on which the opinion is "wholly or substantially based" applies to the facts assumed or observed so as to produce the opinion propounded.

From the criteria above, doubt could raised as to the admissibility of expert opinion from a (solely) vendor certified practitioner. Criteria two is in doubt as it is questionable whether being an expert at using a tool is considered an expert in the field. Criteria six also raises doubt as "the expert's evidence must explain how the field of 'specialised knowledge'... applies to the facts assumed or observed so as to produce the opinion propounded". It is unlikely that such an expert could formulate and justify opinions with such narrow and specific training. It is imperative that standards and certifications be established in forensic computing for the purpose of identifying qualified expert witnesses [7]

3   Available Certifications and Accreditations

Training, certification and accreditation in computer forensics is varied in nature and quality. The difference between certification and accreditation is to whom or to what it applies. Both confirm a certain level of competence in meeting a given set of criteria. Certification applies to an individual such as a computer forensic analyst whereas accreditation applies to an organisation - in this case it will most likely be a forensic laboratory. An accredited computer forensic laboratory guarantees acceptable facilities, a defined process model, appropriately trained, educated and qualified practitioners, and quality assurance measures[8]. Certified practitioners on the other hand, are guaranteed to have a minimum set of KSA's (Knowledge, Skills, and Abilities) that vary depending on the particular certification in that is held.

3.1   Certification in Forensic Computing

The Certified Computer Examiner (CCE) certification is overseen by an organisation called the International Society of Forensic Computer Examiners (ISFCE) (http://www.isfce.com/). ISFCE is a private, for profit organisation and has strict requirements for holders of the certification. There are no prerequisites for attending the course although there is a level of expected knowledge. A multiple-choice test is available online, which can be taken at no cost, designed to test if the applicant has the required knowledge to sit for the course. Some of the more difficult questions in the online test are: (Key Computer Service 2006b)

"While at a DOS or command prompt, how would you delete a file called FILE1?"

"Have you ever connected/disconnected the keyboard, mouse or monitor on a computer?"

"Are the keyboard and monitor connectors the same on a standard PC?"

The level of knowledge required to answer these questions is relatively low and it is likely that the average middle school student could answer these successfully. The course page indicates that the necessary knowledge to become an expert witness is taught in the course[9]. It is questionable whether it is possible to become an expert just by completing a five-day course. There are other certifications available that are of a similar standard. GIAC Certified Forensics Analyst (GCFA) (http://www.giac.org/certifications/security/gcfa.php) involves a five day training course and a test for the approximate cost of $3200.00 (USD); no prior investigation experience or training is necessary.

A brief investigation into certification in more traditional branches of forensics shows a considerably different approach. The International Association for Identification (IAI) (http://www.theiai.org) offers numerous certifications. The 'Bloodstain Pattern Examiner Certification' is one such certification. The first requirement is 40 hours of education in approved workshops. This requirement can be fulfilled in a five-day period, equalling the whole CCE certification course training time. Further to the 40 hours, to obtain the 'Bloodstain Pattern Examiner Certification' the applicant must also have at least three years experience in the field of bloodstain pattern identification and a further 200 hours of study. This accreditation is clearly more complex and thorough than the forensic computing equivalent.

3.2   Higher Education

Higher education in Australia offers little in the way of computer forensic education. No degree program, like a Bachelor of Forensic Computing, or some such similar degree exist. A number of universities in Australia do offer courses that can be taken as an elective during a computer science programme. The University of South Australia (http://www.unisa.edu.au) offers a fourth year course called 'Forensic Computing: Tools, Techniques and Investigations'. The course curriculum covers many of the basic areas of computer forensics including investigation, legal issues, crime scene management, data collection from various operating systems and standard forensic computing tools. Central Queensland University (http://www.cqu.edu.au) includes computer forensics in a network security course, but does not go into detail. The University of Western Sydney (http://www.uws.edu.au/) offers one of the more specialist forensic computing courses available in Australia. It offers a traditional Bachelor of Computer Science with a major in forensic computing. To complete the degree with that particular major there are a number of compulsory courses. 'Computer Forensic Workshop', 'Operating Systems', 'System Administration Programming', 'Information Security', 'Network Security' and 'Information Systems, Ethics and Law' are all required to major in forensic computing. The Canberra Institute of Technology (http://www.cit.act.edu.au) offers an advanced diploma course in forensic computing; the only higher education course that focuses purely on forensic computing. The website asserts that the course will qualify the person for a job as an "investigator specialising in electronic data evidence including electronic fraud, computer crime investigators, and data recovery specialists".

Gottschalk & Liu [10] conducted a survey of higher education institutes offering edification in forensic computing in the USA. They found 32 different forensic computing related programmes including eight two-year diploma programmes, four four-year degree programmes, four master courses, three graduate certificate programmes and 13 non-graduate certificate programmes.

3.3   Law Enforcement Only

Law enforcement training programmes are not open for public attendance as applicants must be affiliated with a law enforcement agency i.e. both sworn and non-sworn officers can attend. The International Association of Computer Investigative Specialists (IACIS) (http://www.iacis.info/iacisv2/pages/home.php) is a not-for-profit organisation in which membership is only open to law enforcement. The agency offers a variety of courses on different topics and at varying lengths. Two-week courses are run annually, called Forensic Training Courses. They allow attendees to obtain grounding in computer forensic. Members attending courses in subsequent years can elect to take more advanced topics rather than the general stream.

Vendor specific software training is often based on a specific tool or set of tools that is run by the company that owns the tools and these are often delivered for Law Enforcement. These courses can be useful in obtaining training in the specific tools but the weaknesses of the tools may not be made evident [11].

3.5   Accreditations

Within the computer forensic discipline very few accreditations are available than can be used for a forensic computing laboratory. There are three main accreditations commonly used in the field including the 'American Society for Crime Laboratory Directors/Laboratory Accreditation Board' (ASCLD/LAB), the National Association of Testing Authorities (NATA) and ISO 17025 (General Requirements for the Competence of Testing and Calibration Laboratories) [2]. ISO 17025 is not specifically a computer forensic laboratory accreditation (or even a general forensic laboratory accreditation) but rather aimed at any laboratory which is involved in testing or calibration. ISO 17025 verifies that laboratories measurement and decisions are accurate, repeatable, believable and verifiable, delivered in a timely manner and all opinions and recommendations are based on a proper process.

The ASCLD/LAB has two different accreditation programmes, ASCLD/LAB-Legacy and ASCLD/LAB-International. The ASCLD/LAB-Legacy accreditation was developed in 1982 but did not formally recognise forensic computing until July 2003 (Barbara 2004). The ASCLD/LAB-International accreditation is an extension of the ISO 17025 standard. The requirements in addition to ISO 17025 are important parts of the Legacy accreditation not covered under ISO 17025 (Barbara 2004; American Society of Crime Laboratory Directors 2006). As of 16 September 2006, there were 317 laboratories accredited under one of the two ASCLD/LAB accreditations, 204 under Legacy and 13 under the International program. Of the 13 ASCLD/LAB-International accredited laboratories, only one is a digital evidence laboratory [12].

The NATA is an Australian based laboratory accreditation that is similar to the ASCLD-International accreditation as it is implemented on top of ISO 17025. It is recorded as being the oldest certification of that type in the world [13]. Unlike the ASCLD accreditations, NATA is used to recognise any type of testing and calibration laboratory, not just forensic orientated facilities. The NATA website lists 35095 laboratories which have achieved accreditation; only 23 of these are information technology facilities, and none of these are digital evidence based (NATA 2006a). At least one forensic computing laboratory in Australia is currently working towards obtaining the standard [14].

It is important to note that individual examiners working within the accredited laboratory are not certified under any of the accreditation mentioned. Examiners do, however, need to be certified and this is commonly done by the accredited organisation using an internal certification programme [15].

4   Discussion and Conclusion

Forensic Computing is making progress towards becoming a solid forensic science. A number of factors have delayed the transition from the unsystematic computer forensics of the past to the modern structure of the field. Although progress is being made, there is still much development to occur before the industry can be regarded in the same way as traditional forensic disciplines like forensic accounting or forensic ballistics. The major problem that has been plaguing the discipline of forensic computing is the lack of standards and formal methodologies. This can largely be attributed to the relative immaturity of the field and has lead to deficiencies in the quality of training, certification and accreditation of practitioners and laboratories within the field. By comparing the available options for training, certification and accreditation to those of traditional branches of forensic science, it is clear that the forensic computing domain is still missing essential elements of cohesion and authority.

The initial lack of standards and formal methodologies has created a problematic environment. Numerous third party and vendor based training and certifications are offered that are aimed at training forensic practitioners to fulfill the market demand caused by those joining the field. This in turn has stunted the development of formal KSA's (Knowledge, Skills and Abilities) for practitioners and methodologies within the field in general. An additional problem with the certification-based model is inequality of those claiming to be experts, and furthermore, those claiming to be qualified to give expert testimony in a court of law. The very definition of an expert must be clarified by an accepted industry standard in order to begin to rectify the problem. Forensic 'experts' are currently testifying in courts and providing opinion evidence that is taken into account by the 'trier of fact'. There must be justification of the ability of the person to provide such evidence in order to maintain an acceptable legal standard.

The problem goes further than just the abilities of the individual forensic practitioner. Digital forensic laboratory accreditation has only recently become available and this is having a positive impact on the maturity of the field. Beckett [14] argues: "the push to validate the filed as a true forensic science is now being driven by these accreditation standards rather than allow the field to develop in the chaotic manner that has been observed over the last decade". Stringent standards must be implemented and maintained in order to obtain and keep such accreditations. This is instrumental in developing a high level of confidence in output from such laboratories.

The development of laboratory standards has recently started to raise the credibility of forensic computing, but there is still progress to be made for training and certification of individual practitioners. There are a variety of different training programmes available and several individual certifications that can be obtained, but no national or international standard proficiency testing currently exists. A lack of such a testing protocol results in no formal method of defining different levels of practitioners and no way to verify a person who claims to be an expert. All other forensic disciplines have formal methodologies, KSA's, national or international bodies to oversee to field and require minimum standards of tertiary education to practice in the field. Digital Forensics is now developing in a positive direction, encouraged by vendor neutral and internationally recognised accreditations for digital evidence laboratories. Certification in digital forensics needs to be replaced with formal tertiary qualifications and proficiency reviews to determine that all practitioners meet minimum KSA's. Certification is likely to continue to play a role within the domain and verify additional skills. A qualified practitioner may obtain a certification as a 'certified EnCase user' that shows knowledge of the tool rather than knowledge of the field as is the current state. Future development in this direction will see digital forensics unequivocally move into the modern age and become a solid and respected science.

References

1. Occupational Health, Safety and Welfare Regulations (SA) 1986.
2. Beckett, J 2006, Personal communication.
3. Meyers, M & Rogers, M 2004, 'Computer Forensics: The Need for Standardization and Certification', International Journal of Digital Evidence, vol. 3, no. 2.

4. Patel, A & Ó Ciardhuáin, S 2000, 'The impact of forensic computing on telecommunications', IEEE Communications Magazine, vol. 38, no. 11, November 2000, pp. 64-67.

5. Australian Law Reform Commission 1985, Opinion Evidence, viewed October 2006, <http://138.25.65.50/au/other/alrc/publications/reports/26/Ch_14.html>.

6. McDougall, R 2006, Exp ert Evidence, updated 5 March 2006, Supreme Court, NSW, viewed 17 September 2006, <http://www.lawlink.nsw.gov.au/lawlink/Supreme_Court/ll_sc.nsf/pages/SCO_mcdougall130204>.

7. G.Shpantzer & T.Ipsen 2002, 'Law Enforcement Challenges in Digital Forensics', paper presented at the Colloquium on Information Systems Security Education.

8. Pollit, MM 2005, Digital Forensic Accreditation, Certification and Standards, National Center for Forensic Science, viewed 22 September 2006, <www.ncfs.org/dcfb/DFCB101205.ppt>.

9. Key Computer Service 2006b, Thank you for your interest in our training, viewed 20 September 2006, <http://www.cce-bootcamp.com/pretest.htm>.

10. Gottschalk, L & Liu, J 2005, 'Computer Forensics Programs in Higher Education: A Preliminary Study', paper presented at the Technical Symposium on Computer Science Education, St Louis, Missouri, USA, Feb 23-27.

11. Kuchta, KJ 2001, 'Learning the Computer Forensic Way', Information Systems Security, vol. 10, no. 5.

12. American Society of Crime Laboratory Directors 2006, Laboratories Accredited by ASCLD/LAB, updated 16 September, 2006, viewed 22 September 2006, <http://www.ascld-lab.org.legacy/aslablegacylabdirectories.html>.

13. NATA 2006, The History of the National Association of Testing Authorities, Australia, viewed September 22 2006, <www.nata.asn.au/index.cfm?objectid=1D70401C-FB17-96FC-3860E377EF629C43>

14. Beckett, J 2005, 'Forensic Computing Experts, Certification and Categorisation of Roles', paper presented at the Colloquium for the Information Systems Security Education - Asia Pacific, Adelaide, Australia.

15. Barbara, JJ 2004, Digital Evidence Accreditation, viewed 22 September 2006, <http://www.forensicmag.com/articles.asp?pid=28>.

Software Assignments for a Course in Secure E-Commerce

Chris Steketee and Phillip Lock

Advanced Computing Research Centre, School of Comp and Info Science
University of South Australia, Mawson Lakes, SA Australia
{Chris.Steketee, Phillip.Lock}@unisa.edu.au

Abstract. This paper describes a course in computer security for advanced undergraduate students in computer science and software engineering. The aim of
the course is to give the student a thorough grounding in the principles and
practice of cryptography and secure network protocols, and in the application of
these to the development of e-commerce applications. An important part of the
learning process is an assignment in which the student develops software for a
specified e-commerce application. The paper describes a number of these assignments that have been run over the past several years, and reflects on the lessons learned.

1 Introduction

The teaching of computer security in undergraduate programmes has struggled to fit
the burgeoning growth in the field into a limited number of course hours. At the University of South Australia, this has been addressed by building an undergraduate Information Security stream into our Computer Science and Software Engineering programmes, including advanced electives. Currently, two advanced electives are
offered: Forensic Computing and Secure E-Commerce, and students can take both,
one or neither, depending on their interests. Our information security stream is described in [1] and has continued to develop in line with re-development of the undergraduate programmes. In accordance with the University's orientation towards producing practically-oriented graduates, the goal is to produce in students a well-
rounded understanding of IT security and an ability to apply this understanding in industry. Foundation courses take a broad view of the field, from both management and
technological perspectives, whereas the advanced electives focus in relatively specialised areas.

Secure E-Commerce is targetted at imparting the understanding and skills needed
for the design and implementation of secure software systems for electronic commerce on public networks such as the Internet and cellular telephone networks. Our
dual intent is to provide a theoretical basis for our student's understanding of security
technologies and at the same time equip them to apply this to secure software development in industry. We aim to impart a practical understanding of the principles of
cryptography, secure network protocols and public key infrastructure. We include detailed coverage of the principal cryptographic algorithms (both symmetric and asym-

Please use the following format when citing this chapter:

Steketee, C., Lock, P., 2007, in IFIP International Federation for Information Processing, Volume 237, Fifth World Conference on Information Security Education, eds. Futcher, L., Dodge, R., (Boston: Springer), pp. 113–120.

metric) and cryptographic protocols, and methods of authentication including the use of smart cards and biometrics. The last part of the course concentrates on the application of these building blocks to the production of secure systems for electronic commerce application areas such as digital rights management and electronic payment. The course is taught by means of lectures (including guest lectures from industry), a software assignment and a literature research assignment, and workshops which are used to support both the lecture and the assignment work.

1.1   The Software Assignment

Bearing in mind the aims of the course, it is important for students to understand how theory translates into practice for system designers and programmers, gaining hands-on experience in the use of standard security libraries as building blocks for a secure system. This is the purpose of the software assignment. The assignment gives students experience in applying the concepts taught in lectures to an e-commerce application by developing a prototype software system. In the course of this assignment, students deal with issues such as secure storage of keys, the choice of encryption algorithms and modes, and the use of a complex API for cryptography – in this case, the Java Cryptographic Extension, JCE [2].

In addition to developing the software, students are required to reflect on its security properties and write a brief security analysis. This helps to teach them that security in software is difficult to achieve, and in particular that achieving a secure system requires more than building a working application.

For this assignment, students are given a specification which typically includes a high-level security and software design, but are left a considerable amount of freedom in the way they implement this. They are given simple programs to get them started on JCE, but are expected to spend time familiarising themselves with the JCE by reading the specifications and browsing the API. These are important skills for software engineers to develop.

1.2   Educational Objectives

Bloom's taxonomy of educational objectives [3] divides cognitive skills into six stages: knowledge, comprehension, application, analysis, synthesis and evaluation.

This assignment concentrates on the application, synthesis and evaluation stages. In the *application* stage, students use their experience of software design and implementation and apply it to the requirements of the specific problem. The *synthesis* stage consists of putting together their knowledge of computer security with the security requirements of the assignment and the building blocks supplied by the Java security libraries on which their solution will depend. In *evaluation*, students show an understanding of the security strengths and weaknesses of the system, by analysing possible security attacks and proposing defences against these attacks.

1.3 Related Work

We are not aware of a course in Secure E-Commerce with the same focus as ours. A number of courses with a similar title focus on protection issues, particularly in relation to web sites, and limit the practical work to laboratory sessions – eg University of Gloucester [4] and Rochester Institute of Technology [5]. The University of Aberdeen's course "Security and Privacy" [6], which is aimed at applications in e-commerce, e-health and e-science, includes some coverage of cryptography and security protocols but this is necessarily limited because of the broader scope of the course.   Royal Holloway offers a complete Masters degree in Information Security [7], with an opportunity to go into topics in much more depth, but there appears to be little emphasis on laboratory or programming work.

In terms of work similar to the assignments described below, a paper by Rawles and Baker [8] presents an approach to teaching students the concepts of Public Key Infrastructure (PKI) and its application to secure e-mail. The emphasis in that paper is on the hands-on experience of setting up a PKI and secure e-mail system. A PKI programming assignment set by Boneh at Stanford [9] bears similarities to two of our assignments: it requires students to develop a chat room with authentication via SSL, including the requirement to set up a PKI. Another secure chat room assignment by Mitchener and Vahdat [10] forms the basis of our own secure chat room assignment.

2 The Assignments

2.1 Mobile Online Music Store

This assignment illustrates security and cryptography concepts by applying them to a mobile-enabled music store with a simple form of Digital Rights Management (DRM). Students are required to produce a prototype of a music store server and client, which enables the user of the client to download, store and play music tracks, while preventing unauthorised use of the downloaded music.

The client is a mobile phone: this has two consequences. Firstly, it adds interest and currency, as music download has only recently become available for mobile phones. Secondly, it illustrates to students the fact that the mobile phone is a more controlled (and often more secure) environment than a standard desktop computer and therefore amenable to different solutions. For pragmatic reasons, the assignment is actually carried out on a normal computer rather than a phone or a phone simulator, but students need to remember in their security analysis that the system being simulated is phone-based.

The design and implementation complexity of the assignment is reduced by specifying that the music store is operated by a mobile phone service provider, that payment for music is added to the user's phone bill, and that access to the music store is restricted to music-store enabled phones provided by the service provider. This means that payment issues can be excluded from the implementation, and that key distribution issues are simplified.

Security and DRM are based on public key cryptography, with each phone having a key pair. Key pairs are assumed to be generated and distributed securely by the service provider before the phone is issued to the customer: the private key is stored on the phone (only), and the music store maintains a database containing the public key of each phone.

When a phone downloads a music track, the music store server encrypts the music to be downloaded with a random session key, encrypts the session key with the public key of the phone, and sends both to the phone, which stores the music in its encrypted form. The phone's keypair therefore provides the basis for both confidentiality of the music download, and copy protection of the downloaded music. An eavesdropper on the network sees the music in encrypted form only, and any copy made of the encrypted file is not playable on another device. The use of this mechanism illustrates to students the use of encryption on network connections, and one approach to providing a simple form of DRM.

Implementation For this assignment, students were required to implement the RSA algorithm from first principles. This showed students that typical public key encryption algorithms are not difficult to implement, and it also provided a good opportunity to discuss the need for a randomised padding scheme such as PKCS #1 and the attacks it is designed to prevent. On the other hand, for symmetric encryption, they were expected to use the JCE: in part to keep the amount of work required to reasonable bounds, and in part to give an insight into the use of cryptographic libraries.

To keep the amount of work to a manageable size, students were given considerable help in the workshops, including Java source code starting points, and discussion time on RSA implementation.

Security Analysis As well as producing an implementation, students were asked to produce a document analysing the security of this system. The specification was couched in broad terms (what are the security threats and attacks, what system design measures are taken against these, what are the biggest threat and easiest attack remaining?). This meant that students needed to think about the security features of the system: those which are inherent in the specification (such as copy protection), those which they may have added in their implementation (such as protection of the private key), and those which are an inherent weakness (such as the need to trust the client software not to reveal secret information). The security analysis serves to remind students that getting a working implementation is only part of the solution.

Lessons Learned This assignment was quite successful and achieved its aims for most students. The great majority were able to produce at least a basic working implementation, and the better students did everything asked for. However many students produced solutions in which secret information, such as passwords and secret keys, were stored on the client unencrypted. The security analysis was less carefully done than the programming despite accounting for 30% of the available marks. This suggests a need to pay more attention in future presentations of the course, on the one hand to secure programming practices, and on the other to the skills needed to analyse the security of, and security gaps in, a system.

Extensions and Variations The assignment lends itself to many extensions and variations. We note here just a few of them. A complementary assignment could be set to deal with the process of secure keypair generation and distribution, which is taken as a given for this assignment. Another extension or complementary assignment could focus on a payment mechanism. An alternative version of the assignment could be based on the use of a PKI, with each party having a public key certificate: this could be the basis for an implementation not limited to a single service provider.

2.2   Public-Key Infrastructure and Secure Email

The purpose of this assignment is to give students hands-on experience implementing a PKI, and writing programs which make use of a PKI in order to achieve secure communication. Students first set up a simple Certificate Authority and produce signed certificates for the communicating parties. They then write application code to achieve secure communication, with the signed certificates in the PKI providing the basis for the security.

The specific communication task in this assignment is a simulation of secure email communication between a bank and its customers. This is of particular relevance in the current environment in which phishing attacks based on email are common, and where Internet banking provides a target which is particularly attractive to the phishers. The task is an illustration to students that it is possible to have email over an insecure network which is secure in terms of both confidentiality and authentication; the choice of a commercial setting is deliberate in order to relate the assignment to the aims of this course.

The PKI in this assignment is one that is targeted for email communication between the bank and its customers. The bank runs a root Certificate Authority (CA) which signs the certificates of all communicating parties (or clients) − these are defined to be bank departments and customers. All parties are assumed to use the same client software (programmed for this assignment by the student) to send and receive secure email, configured to trust the bank's root CA certificate. This leads to a simple PKI, since there is only one CA, and all certificates are signed directly by that CA. A further simplification is that certificate revocation is not included.

In order to send an email, a client needs to have a certificate of its own, and also the certificate of the intended recipient. The sender's private key is used to sign the message and the recipient's public key is the basis for encrypting the message via a random session key. The recipient uses its own private key to decrypt the message, and uses the public key of the sender to verify the signature of the message. The recipient also validates the sender's certificate against the trusted root CA certificate and checks its validity dates.

Implementation Java keystores are a convenient way to store the keypairs and certificates for this assignment. For the Certificate Authority functionality we used the OpenSSL command-line tool [11], which includes a simple CA function. Support was provided in workshops in which the principles of PKI were discussed before they were covered in lectures, in the provision of sample programs to illustrate the use of the JCE for encryption and certificate validation, and in the use of OpenSSL to set up a CA. In order to allow the students to concentrate on the central issues of the assignment, we allowed them to simulate the sending and receiving of secure email by writing and reading disk files, rather than using (say) JavaMail.

Security Analysis The security analysis required for this assignment was specified more explicitly than that for the music store, concentrating on matters like how bank customers are identified and authenticated, the protection against phishing that the use of such a system may provide, and also how secret data such as private keys and passwords are protected.

Lessons Learned Overall, this assignment was less successful than we had hoped. Just two students (10% of the class) completed the work fully and successfully. Despite the considerable amount of help supplied, the others struggled to varying degrees. It is clear that many had difficulties getting to grips with the range of new ideas to learn for this assignment. The main problem may simply have been the complexity of the Java API for cryptography and security, and the students' relative lack of skills in constructing solutions based on the API and simple examples (in terms of Bloom's taxonomy, in the synthesis stage of learning).

Extensions and Variations One area for extensions or complementary assignments is to enhance the PKI functionality, such as adding revocation checking via Certificate Revocation Lists or the OCSP protocol, and generalising to a CA hierarchy with multiple levels. A related extension would be the use of full-function CA software, which would allow the inclusion of certificate revocation and also the periodic re-issue of client certificates. Building a system that sends and receives real emails would be an improvement over simulated email, allowing students to get a clearer picture than they do in an application which is just based on the reading and writing of local files. Variations that apply PKI to some application other than email, for example a payment system, are also possible.

2.3   Secure Chat Room

This assignment requires students to build the infrastructure for secure network communication, and apply it to an Internet chat room application. The basic idea was taken from an assignment published by Mitchener and Vahdat [10]. Students are given an implementation of a chat room application that communicates in plaintext, and are required to convert this to communicate using encrypted messages. Unlike the two assignments described above, this one concentrates on the implementation of a secure protocol, rather than on a specific E-Commerce application.

The protocol which the students are required to implement is essentially a simplified version of Kerberos [12], and is therefore based on symmetric cryptography and the use of a trusted authentication server. Each participant shares a long-term secret key with the authentication server, derived by hashing a password typed in by a user. This is used to authenticate the user and also to encrypt communication with the authentication server. When participant Alice (eg a chat user) wants to communicate with another participant Bob (eg the chat server), Alice requests a ticket from the authentication server: this ticket contains two copies of a newly-generated session key, one encrypted with Alice's long-term key and the other with Bob's long-term key. When Alice opens communication with Bob, she sends Bob's copy of the encrypted session key, and subsequent communication between Alice and Bob is encrypted with this key. The authentication protocol also includes timestamps as a defence against replay attacks.

Implementation Once again students are expected to implement this assignment in Java, using the JCE to perform the cryptographic operations. A plaintext chat room application is supplied as a starting point.

Security Analysis Topics that students were asked to cover in their analysis included the design measures taken to protect long-term keys on the authentication server, secure registration and maintenance of user accounts, and possible attacks, for example the distribution by an attacker of a modified client.

Lessons Learned The assignment was quite successful, with the great majority of students achieving at least a basic working implementation and demonstrating a reasonable understanding in their security analysis. One shortcoming in most solutions was to build the security implementation directly into the chat application rather than encapsulating it in (say) a secure subclass of the *Socket* class.

Variations Clearly the assignment can be adapted to apply the same concepts to other applications needing authentication and encrypted communication. Given our experience noted above, another variation might be to require students explicitly to define and implement a Java API for secure communication based on this protocol, before using it for a specific application.

3   Conclusions

We have described several software design and implementation assignments in which cryptographic techniques are applied to the development of secure applications in an e-commerce environment. These assignments focus on the use of standard implementations of cryptographic algorithms for security purposes rather than on the development of new implementations. The aim is to develop in students a detailed appreciation of the issues involved in developing secure application software, ranging from the nuts and bolts of using a complex cryptographic API, through design issues such as the secure storage of private keys, to an overall security analysis of the system, including remaining security weaknesses. We feel that these assignments have been successful in achieving this aim, in addition to providing students with experience that is valuable for prospective employers.

These assignments have also provided us with a good feedback mechanism on the strengths and weaknesses of our course. One shortcoming that has become apparent is the difficulty many students have in providing a carefully thought-out evaluation of a system's security: while most students are able to produce a standard list of security threats and defences, the ability to analyse threats to a specific software system that they have produced themselves is often lacking. It is clear attention should be paid to this aspect in future presentations. Another lack that has been revealed in the course is the absence of material on secure programming practices, for example to minimise the exposure to a hacker of sensitive information such as passwords and private keys by ensuring that this material is erased from memory after use.

References

1. J. Slay and P. Lock, "Developing an Undergraduate IT Security Stream: Industry Certification and the Development of Graduate Qualities," presented at Fourth World Conference on Information Security Education, WISE4, Moscow, Russia, 2005.
2. Sun Microsystems, "Java Cryptography Extension (JCE) Reference Guide," 2004, http://java.sun.com/j2se/1.5.0/docs/guide/security/jce/JCERefGuide.html, accessed 08/08/2006.
3. B. S. Bloom, Taxonomy of educational objectives. Boston, MA: Allyn and Bacon, 1984.
4. S. A. Shaikh, "Information Security Education in the UK: a proposed course in Secure E-Commerce Systems," presented at 1st Annual Conference on Information Security Curriculum Development, Kennesaw, GA, USA, 2004.
5. Rochester Institute of Technology, "Secure E-Commerce," 2006, http://register.rit.edu/courseSchedule/4002877, accessed 31/10/2006.
6. University of Aberdeen, "Security and Privacy," 2006, http://www.csd.abdn.ac.uk/~jmasthof/teaching/CS5401/, accessed 31/10/2006.
7. R. Holloway, "Master in Information Security," 2006, http://www.isg.rhul.ac.uk/msc, accessed 31/10/2006.
8. P. T. Rawles and K. A. Baker, "Developing a public key infrastructure for use in a teaching laboratory," presented at 4th Conference on Information Technology Curriculum, Lafayette, Indiana, USA, 2003.
9. D. Boneh, "Cryptography and Computer Security: Programming Project #2," 2004, http://crypto.stanford.edu/~dabo/courses/cs255_winter04/, accessed 14/08/2006.
10. W. G. Mitchener and A. Vahdat, "A Chat Room Assignment for Teaching Network Security," presented at 32nd Technical Symposium on Computer Science Education (SIGCSE), 2001.
11. OpenSSL, http://www.openssl.org/, accessed 14/08/2006.
12. B. C. Neumann and T. Ts'o, "Kerberos: An Authentication Service for Computer Networks," IEEE Communications, vol. 32, pp. 33-38, 1994.

Teaching Cryptography to Continuing Education Students

Anatoly Temkin

Department of Computer Science, Metropolitan College, Boston University
808 Commonwealth Avenue, Room 250, Boston, MA 02215, USA
temkin@bu.edu

Abstract. Knowledge of mathematical foundations of Cryptography is of paramount importance for students wanting to succeed in graduate degree programs in Computer Science with concentration in security. Cryptography, a relatively new field, has yet to establish a core set of topics and the optimal sequence of their presentation to prepare students for a career in the field of IT security. This paper presents syllabi of two courses on public and private key cryptography offered to continuing education students at Boston University.

1   Introduction

The Computer Science Department at Boston University Metropolitan College offers, among other degrees and certificates, a Master's in Computer Science with a concentration in security and a graduate certificate in computer security. Cryptography, data communications and computer networks, network security, network management and computer security, software security, and digital forensics are among the courses offered by the department [1]. Cryptography, a two semester course, plays an essential role in the curriculum by serving as a foundation for all other security related courses. Public key cryptography is covered in the first semester followed by private key cryptography in the second semester.

2   Students' Background

Students taking elective courses, and cryptography courses as electives, have a significant amount of programming experience. Some are professional programmers working as developers for software companies. Many students did not major in Engineering, Computer Science or Mathematics in their undergraduate programs, so math courses other than introductions to Calculus and Finite Math were not part of their curriculum They entered the programming field at the end of the last century with majors in history, business, psychology etc and learned programming on the job or by completing certificate programs. By the time they enroll into a Master's degree program in Computer Science, their math background is very weak or almost nonexis-

Please use the following format when citing this chapter:

Temkin, A., 2007, in IFIP International Federation for Information Processing, Volume 237, Fifth World Conference on Information Security Education, eds. Futcher, L., Dodge, R., (Boston: Springer), pp. 121–128.

tent. Students use their working knowledge of programming to grasp new concepts. They try to explain new material in terms of familiar programming concepts.

There are two different types of students in the program: students with a math, computer science, physics or engineering academic background and students without a technical background. Most students from both groups hold full-time programming jobs. In addition to having different academic backgrounds, students vary in their work experience and by the number of years since graduating from college. The average age of students is approximately thirty. Having students with different background in the same classroom presents obvious problems. To make a course successful, we cannot rely on the knowledge students acquired in their undergraduate education, rather we should tailor instructions in a way that will be engaging to all students. Lectures and presentations should be structured to stimulate student interest without overwhelming the student. Overpowering information results in the lack of interest which is necessary to pursue studies. This principal of Zone of Proximal Development was introduced by Vigodsky [3] and is considered to be a major factor in successful education. The problem of keeping a balance between the amount of math in the course on cryptography and the students' ability to understand is a delicate issue. Having taught the course to about 200 students allows me to claim that my careful selection of topics to cover and their presentation order enabled most students' success in a math intensive crypto course.

Of course, there are prerequisite and core courses in the program, like Discrete Mathematics and the Analysis of Algorithms which prepare students to handle mathematical and computational concepts, but there is still a gap between the content of these courses and the abstract content of the group theory. It is not quite clear which crypto topics should be taught to students. Even less clear is the teaching sequence of these topics. For example, should public key or private key cryptography be taught first? We think the answer to this question depends on the objectives set forth before a course is offered. Our objective is to cover mathematical fundamentals of cryptography and that dictates first the coverage of the public key cryptography followed by the private key cryptography. We believe that the content of our courses on cryptography prepares students for successful work in the field.

Next, we introduce the two course sequences on cryptography

3   A Course on Public Key Cryptography.

Despite its name, the course on public key cryptography is not only on encryption theory but also on cryptanalysis. The course begins with a review of the number theory, paying special attention to the unique factorization of integers into primes, the Euclidean Algorithm for finding the greatest common divisor of two integers and its extension to finding multiplicative inverses modulo n. Basic group theory is reviewed and extended with thorough discussion of the multiplicative groups Z_p for p prime and Z_n for a composite n, which are used in the ElGamal and the RSA ciphers. Subgroups, Lagrange Theorem, Euler and Fermat Theorems, index of a subgroup and cyclic subgroups are among the basic facts about groups covered. Having familiarized students with the basic ideas, the next step is a deeper coverage of groups, including, but not limited to, roots and powers in groups. This allows introducing the definition of a discrete logarithm followed by the ElGamal cipher along with some algorithms to compute discrete logs in cyclic groups. The algorithms presented are the Baby-step Giant-step algorithm and the Index Calculus method. The second part of the course begins with a thorough coverage of the RSA cipher. The AlGamal cipher is followed by the RSA cipher along with a discussion of various attacks, such as forward search, common modulus and small decryption exponent. Right after the RSA cipher several important protocols are covered, more specifically secret sharing, oblivious transfer and zero-knowledge proofs. Quadratic Reciprocity is introduced to present Euler probabilistic primality test. Along with Fermat, Euler and Rabin-Miller pseudo-primes the corresponding algorithms are covered. Random number generators, including Blum-Blum-Shub and Naor-Reingold generators are discussed in detail. In the third part of the course much attention is devoted to factorization attacks. Although this material requires a certain amount of mathematical preparation, not all of which is required of our students, with a certain diligence it is quite possible not to just explain the concepts but to carry them through to the practical algorithmic implementation. Pollard's Rho Method along with Pollard's $p-1$ method is presented. Among modern factorization attacks most attention is devoted to Dixon and the Quadratic Sieve algorithms. The primary texts for this course are textbooks [4] and [5] supplemented with lecture notes. The course is in the lecture format with weekly homework assignments and final projects.

Students are required not only to understand in depth theoretical foundations of the subject matter, but also to utilize their programming skills to write codes for algorithms used in breaking cryptographic codes. Our belief is that once students learn the ideas behind algorithms used in breaking codes they will be much better prepared to understand how to securely implement these algorithms.

The assignments for each of the lectures include problem solving and code writing. All algorithms covered in the course have to be coded by students and the final project is based on the previously coded algorithms. Among algorithms covered in the course are Euclidean and the extended Euclidean algorithms to find multiplicative inverses modulo n, the fast exponentiation algorithm, a primitive root search algorithm, a Baby-step Giant-step and the Index calculus algorithms to find Discrete Logarithms in Cyclic groups, a Miller-Rabin test, Naor-Reingold and Blum-Blum-Shub random number generator algorithms, Pollard's Rho, Pollard's $p-1$ and the Quadratic Sieve factoring algorithms.

For two final projects the class is broken into groups of three students [2]. For the first project, if A, B and C are students in a group, then each of them encrypts two messages using the Diffie-Hellman Key Exchange Protocol and sends them to other members of the same group. That is, A encrypts a message and sends it to B, while C, the adversary, tries to break this message by using Baby-step algorithm and the Index Calculus algorithms to find discrete logs in cyclic groups. Then A encrypts another message and sends it to C, while B, the adversary, tries to break into the message by using the same algorithms. Then B and C encrypt their messages and the whole process is repeated. So every member of a group is involved in encoding two messages and recovering two messages as an adversary.

For the second project, the same members of a group are involved in the exchange of messages within the same scheme using the RSA algorithm. They use the Pollard's Rho algorithm, Pollard's $p \square 1$ method and Quadratic Sieve algorithm to break into the messages.

Here is a syllabus for the course on public key cryptography with some comments

Week 1: Integers, prime numbers, relatively prime numbers, greatest common divisors, factorization into prime numbers, computation of $\square (n)$ based on Principle of Inclusions and Exclusions, the Euclidean and the Expanded Euclidean Algorithms, multiplicative inverses, equivalence relations, classes of integers modulo n, defining binary operations of addition and multiplication on classes of integers modulo n.

Comments: Operations of addition and multiplication are defined on Z_n before a formal definition of a group is introduced. The definition comes in the second lecture and Z_n and $Z_n^{\square}$ serve as examples of groups.

Week 2: Definition of a group, examples of groups (finite and infinite), groups Z_n and $Z_n^{\square}$, subgroups, cosets, Lagrange Theorem, cyclic groups, the exponent of a group, Euler and Fermat theorems.

Comment: I consider it very important to cover the introduction into the group theory as soon as possible in the course. My experience from teaching this course to about 200 students in the last four years supports this practice.

Week 3: Exponentiation Algorithm, Primitive Roots, Discrete Logs, ElGamal Cipher

Comments: A discrete log problem is introduced in an abstract group as well as the ElGamal cipher. In the following week lecture this cipher is run in $Z_p^{\square}$

Week 4: The Diffie-Hellman Key Exchange Protocol, Primitive Root Search Algorithm, Baby-Step Giant-Step Algorithm, The Index Calculus Algorithm Public-Key Ciphers.

Comments: It seems very important not just to explain ciphers but to introduce probabilistic algorithms used to break ciphers.

Week 5: Introduction to Public Key ciphers, The RSA Cipher and attacks on RSA. Key distribution, mutual authentication, certificates.

Week 6: Chinese Remainder Theorem, Euler Criterion, Roots Mod Composites.

Week 7: Oblivious Transfer Protocol (factorization and discrete log based). Zero-knowledge proofs, authentication.

Week 8: Quadratic Reciprocity.

Week 9: Pseudorandom numbers, Fermat, Euler, and strong pseudoprimes, Solovay-Strassen test, Miller-Rabin test.

Week 10: Random Number generators, Linear Congruential generator, Feedback Shift generator, Noar-Reingold Generator, Blum-Blum-Shub Generator

Week 11: Modern Factorization Attacks. Pollard's Rho Method, Pollard's p-1 Method

Week 12: Dixon's algorithm, Non-Sieving Quadratic Sieve, The Quadratic Sieve Factoring Algorithm.

4   A Course on Private Key Cryptography.

The second semester course on private key cryptography begins with a thorough introduction into the theory of finite fields with coverage of commutative rings, irreducible elements of rings, group of units, the Euclidean algorithm in a polynomial ring, fields Z_p and $GF(2^m)$. The coverage continuous with the ring of polynomials mod P, operations of addition, multiplication and finding inverses in that ring. Discussing finite fields is important for the in-depth coverage of DES and Whirlpool hash function. The course goes on with the coverage of encryption systems and attacks against them. Fiestel ciphers and DES are discussed in detail. A lot of attention in lectures is given to block cipher modes of operation and hash functions based on block ciphers.

Security of hash functions, iterated hash functions, message authenticated codes are covered along with digital signatures and authentication protocols. Public Key Infrastructure, certificates, trust models, IP security protocols, Transport Layer Security/Secure Sockets Layer protocols are discussed by the end of the course and, finally, an introduction into elliptic curves and ElGamal public key encryption is covered.

The primary texts for this course are textbooks [4], [5], [6] and [7] supplemented with lecture notes. The course is in the lecture format with weekly homework assignments and a final project. Homework assignments include writing codes for the algorithms covered and the final project. For the final project, students are broken in groups of two. If A and B are in the same group, A encrypts a message using AES, hashes it, "signs" it and sends the encrypted message and its signature to B. B verifies both the authenticity of the message and its integrity and decrypts it. Then A and B switch roles.

Here is a syllabus for the course on private key cryptography with some comments.

Week 1: Rings, commutative rings, zero divisors and integral domain, cancellation property in a commutative ring, irreducible elements of a ring, the additive group of a ring, the group of units, fields, polynomial rings, the Euclidean algorithm in a polynomial ring over a field.

Week 2: Finite fields, fields Z_p, congruence classes of a polynomials modulo P, irreducible polynomials of degree n, the ring of polynomials mod P as a finite field, field extensions; addition, multiplication and multiplicative inverses in the ring of polynomials mod P.

Week 3: Advanced Encryption Standard block cipher.

Comments: For some reasons students think that whatever the mathematical apparatus used for public key cryptography is totally different from the one used for private key cryptography. It is very important to emphasize the mathematical foundations of block ciphers like AES, to go over a group $GF(2^8)$, irreducible polynomials, inverse elements etc.

Week 4: Encryption schemes, unconditionally, computationally and provably secure encryption systems, attacks against the encryption scheme (ciphertext only, known-plaintext and chosen-plaintext, chosen ciphertext), a simple substitution cipher, polyalphabetic ciphers, block and stream ciphers, the Vernam cipher, a one-time pad.

Fiestel ciphers and DES. Linear and differential cryptanalysis.

Week 5: The New Data Seal (NDS) cipher and a chosen-plaintext attack on NDS. Tweakable block ciphers and modes of operation: Tweak Block Chaining, Tweak Chain Hash and Tweakable Authenticated Encryption.

Comments: As NDS uses the same key in all rounds, the chosen-plaintext attack is successful and although NDS is never used in "real" life situations, it is beneficial for students to learn how the key is recovered as the result of the attack.

Week 6: Double DES, its vulnerability to meet-in-the-middle attack, triple DES, block cipher modes of operations. Electronic codebook (ECB), Cipher-block chaining(CBC), cipher feedback (CFB), Output feedback (OFB), Counter (CTR). Error propagation, integrity protection.

Week 7: One way functions, trapdoor functions, confidentiality and non-repudiation, hash functions, properties of cryptographic hash functions (preimage, second preimage and collision resistance), the random oracle model. Iterated hash functions, the Matyas-Meuer-Oseas and Miyaguchi-Preneel hash function constructions. The Mercle-Damgard generic construction of cryptographic hash functions. The Digital Signature Algorithm

Week 8: A Whirlpool cryptographic hash function. Coverage of MD-4, MD-5, SHA1, SHA-256, 384, 512, a commitment scheme and verification of message integrity.

Comments: The coverage of a Whirlpool hash function seems to be important as the hash function's construction is based on a block cipher similar to AES.

Week 9: Message authentication codes, message authentication codes built from block ciphers, HMACs, Swcurity of MACs, vulnerability of MACs to birthday, collision and other attacks.

Week 10: Public Key Infrastructure, certificates, trust models, IP security protocols, Transport Layer Security/ Secure Sockets Layer protocols

Week 11: Introduction into elliptic curves over finite fields Z_p and F_q, a group operation on an elliptic curve, points at infinity.

Comments: This material seems to be the most difficult for students since it is math intensive. However, most students grab the concept of elliptic curves and are prepared to further their knowledge through independent reading.

Week 12: Elliptic curve cryptography: ElGamal public key encryption, Massey-Omura encryption, ElGamal Digital Signatures, the Digital Signature Algorithm.

5   Conclusion

Students' feedback is highly encouraged and plays a significant role in the design and updates of the crypto course. Being academic in nature, this course has the potential to make an immediate impact on students' ability to utilize the knowledge gained in the classroom in their professions. Since many students taking this class work full-time for leading companies in the security field, like RSA Security and Cisco, or are employed as computer security professionals at other companies, very often holding leading positions, their opinion of course content and its modes of offering is very valuable. Students' satisfaction with the course on security as well as their satisfaction with the whole program is a litmus test for the faculty. A large number of students consider the course on cryptography to be highly challenging but manageable. There should be a significant effort on the part of the student to learn. The efficacy of the course is conveyed in almost every student's evaluation. Working professionals always evaluate courses based on how much they learn and on the amount of applicability to their immediate line of work. I am listing some of the student's feedback comments.

"The usage of this class will help me evaluate the security we can build into our Web services, our password encryption in particular. The understanding of cracking the codes for the RSA and the Diffie-Hellman key exchange will help me choose good keys for these secure communication protocols."

"I work as a systems integration engineer in the International Air Traffic Control division. My responsibilities are to help engineers integrate radar software and hardware components. Two years ago, I made the decision to pursue my Master's degree in Computer Science with specialization in security. At work with the proliferation of networks and the internet, increasingly security is playing a prominent role in every aspect of the projects I have worked on. The cryptography course helped me a great deal to get a better understanding and appreciation for the role and benefits of application, system and network security.

I feel compelled if not obligated to learn more about security in order to perform my job adequately. I find myself increasingly involved in the role of a security engineer which requires a strong understanding of cryptography. I have enjoyed and learned a lot from the Cryptography class and I believe it is the most important course in computer science degree program with security concentration."

"I think that I have re-learned how to think, especially in a course environment! So, this will be of tremendous value as I continue with other courses in the program. I anticipate that I will have a focus in security as part of my responsibilities as an integrated solution architect within the next year. My role is evolving and as the focus integration within the healthcare enterprise increases, the security will become important and the ability to exchange shared secrets for use in secure communications will be essential. I will need to have an understanding of what options are available and the tradeoffs between them. Having the understanding of the mathematical foundations for the protocols will be helpful to truly understand how the protocols should be used and how they might be compromised."

"As far as my professional work is concerned, the course has opened my eyes to the hazards of believing we are "secure". The cryptography course, more than anything, has piqued my interest in math. I kept telling my friends all semester that cryptography is the best math class I had ever taken. As an aside, the project may be one of the most fun projects I've ever had for a course. We have had quite a good time going back and forth trying to break RSA private keys. It's amazing how big these numbers can get yet we are still able to crack them. But it's also incredible to see how well-chosen keys resist Rho, p-1, and other attacks!"

"My role at work is to design and develop our company's IT infrastructure, especially around networks and security. While I've always been considered one of the most security-conscious employees on the team, it wasn't until this course that I fully came to appreciate the importance of cryptography. For example, in the past when evaluating a vendor's product, I'd have been satisfied to learn "encryption" was available. Given what I now know today, this wouldn't be enough - e.g. what specific encryption algorithms are being used? Who developed the encryption protocols (i.e. in-house vs. standard, well-known protocols like RSA)? What key-length is being used? I'll want to understand the specifics to ensure that choices we make as a company are well-informed and grounded in a strong technological basis and not on marketing hype."

"I found this course very valuable in truly understanding how crypto works while working in a security environment. By making this more a course in cryptology and using real-world examples the student is given a solid education."

"In this class I have learned much of the mathematical basis for algorithms that I use in my professional work. It is helpful to understand the underpinnings for RSA and Diffie -Hellman protocols as that will enable me to make better use of them and avoid pitfalls that I otherwise might encounter.

"I had an interest in finite fields in high school, but had no idea about what applications there might exist. This course has re-stimulated my interest in this field and particularly cryptology. I have a special interest in (t,n)-threshold schemes and new uses for cryptography. I'm also especially interested in provably secure pseudorandom number generators, how pseudorandom number generators can be evaluated, and what it means for something to actually be, or appear to be, random. I spent a lot of time working on my final projects; building the rudiments of a "Cryptologic Workbench" that I hope will help me explore some of these ideas more thoroughly. I also have some ideas on how a scalable web services-enabled cryptologic workbench might enable a larger community to cooperatively explore these ideas.

References

1. Zlateva, T et al. Integrated Curricula for Computer and Network Security Education, Proceedings of the Colloquium for Information Systems Security Education, Society for Advancing Information Assurance and Infrastructure Protection, Washington, D.C., June 2003.
2. Chitkushev, L.T. et al. Laboratory Assignments in Security Education, Proceedings of the 4th World Conference on Information Security Education. Editors: Natalia Miloslavskaya, Helen L. Armstrong. Success Through Information Security Knowledge, IFIP TC11 / WG11.8 Forth World Conference on Information Security Education (WISE 4), June 18-20, 2005, Moscow, Russia. ISBN 5-7262-0565-0
3. Vygotsky, L.S., Mind in Society: The Development of Higher Psychological Processes, Cambridge, Mass: Harvard University Press, 1978
4. Garrett, P. Making, Breaking Codes: An Introduction to Cryptology. Upper Saddle River, NJ: Prentice Hall, 2001
5. Stallings W. Cryptography and Network Security: Principles and Practices, 4th edition.Upper Saddle River, NJ: Prentice Hall, 2006
6. Washington, Lawrence C. Elliptic Curves, Number Theory and Cryptography, Chapman & Hall/CRC 2003
7. Stinson, Douglas R. Cryptography: Theory and Practice, 3d edition, Chapman & Hall/CRC 2006

The Role of Mathematics in Information Security Education

Stephen D. Wolthusen[1,2]

[1] Gjøvik University College, N-2802 Gjøvik, Norway,
stephen.wolthusen@hig.no
[2] Royal Holloway, University of London, Egham TW20 0EX, United Kingdom,
stephen.wolthusen@rhul.ac.uk

Abstract. There exists a disconnect between the expectations of students of information security and the requirements imposed on their mathematical abilities and maturity at both the M.Sc. and Ph.D. levels. In this paper we discuss efforts at Gjøvik University College, Norway, to bridge this gap on one hand by providing a targeted curriculum component intended to provide the necessary mathematical tools for conducting research at the doctoral level. On the other hand we are critically examining the curricular dependencies and requirements at the M.Sc. level where two factors are becoming evident. First, not all students at this level have adequate mathematical backgrounds to be able to profit fully from the program even though they may meet all formal prerequisites. Second, there may exist areas where the depth and rigor of the mathematical foundations currently in place in the curriculum is not be strictly necessary. Both of these factors can impede access and subsequent success of graduate programs and must therefore be addressed carefully with the aim of striking a balance between these competing objectives.

1 Introduction

The appeal of information security as a subject of studies at the graduate level transcends the core areas of computer science and mathematics, particularly in case of M.Sc. studies where the objectives of students may be more oriented towards improving their insight into pragmatic questions rather than towards academic research questions [1].

As a result of this broad appeal, it can be observed that the mathematical background knowledge, skills, and maturity vary considerably for students entering M.Sc. degree programs in information security, even though formal requirements have been met. Reasons for this diversity include that students may have been enrolled in undergraduate degree programs which placed a different emphasis, e.g. a curriculum oriented more towards calculus instead of discrete mathematics and theoretical computer science in case of students from engineering programs.

In other cases students enter the program with significant work experience that did not exercise their mathematical skills acquired earlier, resulting in students that are formally qualified but whose capabilities have atrophied. A key

Please use the following format when citing this chapter:

Wolthusen, S., 2007, in IFIP International Federation for Information Processing, Volume 237, Fifth World Conference on Information Security Education, eds. Futcher, L., Dodge, R., (Boston: Springer), pp. 129–136.

challenge is therefore to provide a curriculum which can bridge these diverse levels of preparedness, inclination, and skill while maintaining sufficient rigor [2].

Research students at the doctoral level present a different set of challenges. While these research-oriented students typically do not take a utilitarian approach as may be the case for M.Sc. students who – rightfully – see the mathematical foundations of information security as only one tool of many to equip them to solve problems in what is typically an application domain, the nature of information security research as a cross-cutting concern implies a need for an equally broad theoretical background depending on the research interests of individual students.

While in some cases it may be possible to approach these problems to requiring completion of core courses in mathematics and theoretical computer science, the density and interdependencies within the study programs make such an approach problematic and potentially wasteful (see also [3] for a recent survey of approaches to information security program organization). A more targeted integration of the requisite foundations holds several potential advantages. First and foremost, the material can be presented in a more targeted manner unencumbered by the traditions in some areas which, while essential to the understanding of the area as a whole for research mathematicians, tend to include elements of limited interest when dealing with the typically more applied problems faced by students of information security. A second advantage inherent in this focused approach in that it allows a tighter integration into core information security curricula.

By ensuring that key concepts, e.g. from complexity and computability theory or number-theoretical foundations, which are required in several core curriculum components, are covered in such a way to both reinforce the concepts on one hand and to minimize the need for redundant yet, owing to its necessary brevity, superficial treatment of such material, it becomes possible to maintain a sufficiently challenging depth of coverage while at the same time providing a stronger motivation for interacting with these foundations since the curriculum helps to see interconnections and interdependencies which may be lost when covered in a more linear and independent manner. This, however, can only succeed if students view these foundations not merely as part of an isolated part of the curriculum (i.e. primarily cryptography courses) but rather as an integral and in many ways unifying element which is key to achieving a deeper understanding of the subject matter.

The remainder of this paper is structured as follows: Section 2 reviews opportunities and challenges for integrating appropriate reviews and elaborations on mathematical foundations into a M.Sc. curriculum which must take the diverse backgrounds and ultimately also the objectives of students into account. Section 3 then discusses the mathematical coursework for doctoral students either mandatory or recommended regardless of the specialization individual students are pursuing. The course offerings along with the motivation for their provision for the more specialized areas of interest are then detailed in section 4, with section 5 providing a summary of the experience to date and an outlook on further reviews and refinements to the proposed curriculum.

2   M.Sc. Level Foundations

As noted in section 1, the core problems requiring careful attention in providing a rigorous and solid theoretical foundation to information security studies at the M.Sc. level stem primarily from the diversity of backgrounds and, to a lesser extent, the diverging objectives students have for entering a dedicated degree program at the M.Sc. level without necessarily wishing to pursue further studies at the doctoral level [4].

The latter manifests itself primarily in a need to continuously motivate the inclusion of theoretical foundations with a clear perspective on the implications of such results and techniques. These can either be found immediately in applications, or can be motivated by emphasizing the cross-connections made possible by applying similar mathematical techniques in areas which at least at first seem disparate. The former issue, however, cannot be addressed entirely within the confines of the regular curriculum. By offering optional summer course modules in key areas of mathematics, students are given the opportunity to gain or refresh the requisite background and dexterity in applying mathematical techniques which can yield a comparable point of departure for all students beginning the program.

Several aspects need to be considered in structuring these offerings in addition to the content itself and must take the learning experiences and expectations of students into account. For students entering into the M.Sc. program, the learning techniques and strategies acquired before entering the program will differ markedly. Students entering the program directly after completing and undergraduate degree may, depending on their previous field of study, have an advantage over mature students, which are typically mid-career professionals released, often on a part-time basis, by their employers or are re-training in that they have skills more readily at their disposal, e.g. in performing calculations or algebraic transformations.

However, regardless of student background, several key techniques are often only inadequately developed except in case of students entering from an undergraduate program in mathematics, the most important of which is the concept of rigorous proof and a selection of proof techniques and heuristics. While even an intense summer program is insufficient to impart the dexterity in using these techniques one would need for approaching novel problems, the requirements in the information security program are more modest and focused. Based on an adequate degree of familiarity, students are enabled to both follow proof arguments and to explore minor variations and extensions to existing theorems on their own.

The preparatory summer course then provides a compact overview of several areas required as background for the mandatory and most elective courses offered within the M.Sc. program itself and is also recommended for students having covered this material in their previous studies. Since an introduction to cryptography is mandatory, this necessarily includes elements of number theory. Topics covered include the ring of integers (refined further in the segment on abstract algebra), congruences, and rings of integers modulo u. Selected algorithms covered include the Chinese Remainder Theorem and Fermat's Little Theorem for prime modulus together with Euler's generalization to arbitrary moduli, primitive roots and quadratic residues along with an introduction to the problem of factorization of large integers. This then leads to a coverage of core concepts from abstract algebra, including functions and relations, groups along with cyclic and permutation groups and homomorphisms. In addition, selected aspects of the properties of commutative rings and fields along with structures of groups are discussed, which naturally leads to a brief introduction to Galois theory.

Several M.Sc. modules also require familiarity with elementary probability and statistics; this is reflected in the coverage of probability models, conditional and unconditional probability, random variables, and probability distribution models in the preparatory course. Other requirements of several modules include basic combinatorics and set theory, together with an overview of topics in computability and complexity.

Mandatory core modules on cryptography and the theory of information security can then build on these common foundations without excessive repetition, with the former relying on the on the number theoretic, algebraic, and combinatorial background and the latter relying on the material on computability and complexity, abstract algebra, and probability theory. In addition, elective courses such as those on intrusion detection and authentication also can refer back to the common mathematical background while concentrating on the actual applications of this foundational material.

3   Common Elements for Doctoral Studies

The role of course offerings for doctoral studies is primarily intended as guidance and for providing the requisite background and intellectual tools for the conduct of research, therefore frequently concentrating on foundational aspects at the expense of more concrete research-related issues as the latter is more appropriately covered in the course of seminars and reading groups since this format allows a more immediate adaptation to current research and requirements of the doctoral students.

The mandatory modules for doctoral students in information security are therefore (in addition to modules on "Ethics and Legal Aspects of Scientific Research" and "Methodology of Scientific Research", which are beyond the scope of this paper) focusing on mathematical tools and approaches which can be adapted to the specific research needs. The first module, entitled "Discrete Mathematics" provides an introductory survey of discrete mathematical tools that students primarily interested in applications will require and is also intended to assist students entering the Ph.D. program from courses of study in which discrete mathematics was not a core part of the curriculum. In the course, a rigorous introduction to core topics of abstract algebra is provided through an introduction to linear algebra. The second part of the course is concerned with the introduction of key concepts of combinatorics, including aspects of graph theory and its applications. A second mandatory module which, however, may be substituted by another if a student can demonstrate that it will not be required in his or her particular research is entitled "Applied Statistics". Since this area represents a key tool in a number of areas of applied computer science, particularly where simulations and experiments are conducted and appropriate inferences and hypotheses must be derived, it is integrated into the core Ph.D. curriculum. In this course, the fundamental aspects of probability theory and mathematical statistics including the central limit theorem are covered before moving on to studies of techniques and approaches to modeling and inference, supplemented by fundamental aspects of stochastic processes. Based on this, students can then choose further specialized modules relevant to their research as detailed in the following secction 4.

4   Research Specializations at the Doctoral Level

The research of doctoral students falls into three broad categories, each of which in turn require different supporting modules providing the appropriate mathematical background. This is required for two reasons. First, Gjøvik University College does not have a separate graduate program in mathematics, and so must provide courses from within the information security program. This, however, provides a benefit simular to those described in section 2 for the M.Sc. program in thad secondly, it allows a more targeted approach in the construction of the individual modules to better support the needs of information security students.

The categories can be characterized as:

1. Purely theoretical information security or cryptography
2. Experimental information security
3. Research involving modeling and simulation

It is obvious that there will be research which requires more specialized mathematical background; this, however, is not the focus of the common foundations concept discussed here and is more properly addressed by individual research on the part of the Ph.D. student.

The mathematical background in support of the general research areas is concentrated mainly in the form of lectures as seminars tend to focus more on the concrete applications to information security (although e.g. in cases such as a seminar on "Cryptographic Primitives" and some lectures, the distinction may well be arbitrary). This has led to the identification of the following lecture and seminar modules:

4.1   Computational Methods and Complexity

This course encompasses the core models and mechanisms required for the design and analysis of algorithms and particularly computational models. To this end, models of computation, Turing machines, recursive functions, Church's thesis, λ calculi, decidability, and computability, are covered. Beyond this core, denotational semantics and the logic of programs are covered as well as applications to automata, formal languages, program verification, and programming languages. A final component of the course provides an overview of complexity theory including analytical techniques and an introduction to complexity hierarchies.

4.2   Advanced Graph Theory and Combinatorics

The course begins with classical combinatorics, including counting functions (arbitrary, injective or surjective functions with domain and range either distinguishable or indistinguishable) and enumerations (sets, multisets, permutations, multiset permutations, partitions, set partitions, and compositions). Applications to Bell numbers, Stirling numbers of the first and second kinds, and Eulerian numbers are covered as well as the recurrence relations and bijective methods in proofs. Algebraic techniques covered include generating functions, particularly ordinary and exponential generating functions and applications to to partition problems. Gaussian polynomials are covered in connection with partitions, the lattice of subspaces of a vector space over a finite field, and the q-binomial Theorem.

This course also covers core aspects of graph theory and combinatorics. Beginning with Hamiltonian and Euler circuits and flows including the Max-Flow Min-Cut theorem, integral flows and Menger's theorem, approaches to extremal problems are examined together with selected aspects of Ramsey theory and representation mechanisms. Graph topologies as well as both random and power-law graphs are covered along with selected tools on graph morphology.

4.3   Pattern Recognition

In this course, fundamental aspects of classification techniques are covered, including both parametric and nonparametric techniques. Specific approaches and techniques discussed include linear classifiers and support vector machines, multilayer neural networks, stochastic classification methods that include genetic algorithms and simulated annealing, as well as unsupervised learning and clustering, while emphasizing the connections to applied statistics.

4.4   Computation in Number Theory and Elliptic Curves

This course is primarily intended for students interested in cryptography and covers elements of computational number theory and particularly elliptic curves. Areas covered include a detailed analysis of the Extended Euclidean algorithm and the Montgomery method, deterministic primality testing, generators in $\mathbb{Z}_p^*$, arithmetic over polynomial and finite fields.

5   Conclusions

In this paper we have presented a proposed curriculum structure which deliberately concentrates the mathematical foundations and prerequisite material for research in information security with the aim of striking an appropriate balance between accessibility and rigor.

We believe that the inclusion of these theoretical foundations are an essential prerequisite for conducting successful research not only in the theory of information security and related areas such as cryptography but also in quantitative and applied areas. At the same time we recognize that, particularly at the M.Sc. level, students expect to be exposed to applied and immediately applicable material which they can leverage directly in their subsequent career. At the same time, there appears to be a strengthening negative correlation between the perceived (mathematical) rigor of a degree program and the uptake by students.

It is therefore incumbent on degree programs such as the one we describe to provide a compelling argument for the retention of the theoretical background of information security in the curriculum instead of cutting back on this apparent impediment to student uptake of the degree programs. The key argument we see in favor of the more rigorous and mathematically oriented curriculum is that it enables students to see interconnections and common patterns more clearly, particularly if the courses are designed to strengthen such discovery and analysis. While such a bespoke approach may not be feasible in environments below a certain size or where graduate-level mathematics courses are provided as a service from an established mathematics department, both constraints are not present in case of Gjøvik University College, enabling the development of a mathematics and theory curriculum intended first and foremost to support the core information security curriculum.

As research foci and student requirements change, this curriculum will require constant adjustment to maintain this balance, e.g. also in response to an increased intake of students at both the M.Sc. and Ph.D. levels from countries in which, even though formal degree equivalence may be given, the relevant undergraduate programs may have placed the relative emphasis on different areas. Above all, however, the curriculum must evolve in response to the objective requirements of students and, at the M.Sc. level based on longitudinal surveys of graduates.

Acknowledgments The author would like to thank E. Hjelmås, H. Engenes, J. Gonzalez, S. Petrović, E. Snekkenes, and C.-H. Tan for valuable discussiona and comments.

References

1. Hjelmås, E., Wolthusen, S.: Full-Spectrum Information Security Education: Integrating B.Sc., M.Sc., and Ph.D. Programs. In: Proceedings of the 3rd Annual Conference on Information Security Curriculum Development, Kennesaw, GA, USA, ACM, ACM Press (2006) 9–16

2. Hentea, M., Dhillon, H.S., Dhillon, M.: Towards Changes in Information Security Education. Journal of Information Technology Education **5** (2006) 221–233
3. Taylor, C., Shumba, R., Walden, J.: Computer Security Education: Past, Present and Future. In: Proceedings of the Seventh Workshop on Education in Computer Security (WECS7). (2006) 67–78
4. Ciechanowicz, C., Martin, K.M., Piper, F., Robshaw, M.J.B.: Ten Years of Information Security Masters Programmes. In: World Conference on Information Security Education. (2003) 215–230

The Role of Information Security Industry Training and Accreditation in Tertiary Education

Helen Armstrong[1], Colin Armstrong[2]

[1] Curtin University, Hayman Road, Bentley, Western Australia
[2]Gailaad Pty Limited, Perth, Western Australia
[1]H.Armstrong@cbs.curtin.edu.au
[2]ColinArmstrong@gailaad.net.au

Abstract. This paper presents a proposal for a working group session on the role of industry training and professional certification in information security education at the tertiary level. The main question posed is *Does industry training and professional certification have a place in university information security courses?* If so, *What industry training and professional accreditation courses are appropriate?* and *What is the place of these in academic courses and why?* The discussion will centre on three areas: first, the nature of the linkage between industry requirements and academic offerings at university, and secondly the relevance of industry training and professional certification, and thirdly, the role industry training and certification should play in information security university courses.

Keywords: Information security education, information security industry training, information systems professional certification.

1 Introduction

The relevance of industry training and certification materials in tertiary level information security courses has been a matter of regular discussion over the recent past, with most of the written debate published in conference proceedings. Fueled by diminishing government funding for tertiary education institutions and a desire by computing and professional organizations to increase adoption of their products, the character of information systems and information security education is changing.

Alan Stanley in his invited talk at the SEC 97 conference discussed the changing nature of information security and its increasing challenges in meeting the needs of business in a rapidly changing technological environment. Stanley states the complexity and depth of coverage of the information security area as applied in business "is one of the most intellectually challenging topics"[1].

The NSA in the USA has recently published their desire to recognize US institutions that have plotted their information assurance curriculum to US standards

Please use the following format when citing this chapter:

Armstrong, H., Armstrong, C., 2007, in IFIP International Federation for Information Processing, Volume 237, Fifth World Conference on Information Security Education, eds. Futcher, L., Dodge, R., (Boston: Springer), pp. 137–140.

[2]. This is certainly an incentive for US tertiary institutions to align their educational content with national standards. There is evidence of an increased level of alignment of information assurance curricula with industry training, standards and professional bodies (both national and international). Specific examples can be found in the discussions of Rasmussen & Irvine [3], Armstrong & Murray [4], Klevenger & Alexander [5], Taylor, Alves-Foss & Freeman [6], Schembari [7], and Slay [8].

The lack of security in computerized systems and processes that surround those systems has been the focus of extensive discussion for several decades. In the quest to achieve more secure information systems Conti and others [9] state we must provide the appropriate information security education to the people who have to build these systems.

In the experience of Rasmussen and Irvine [3] the education and experience of the personnel involved in product certification and accreditation is critical. They state that qualified personnel are in short supply and in response have established an educational program for certifiers in their DoD environment which includes qualifying for numerous professional body certifications.

The lack of industry-standard skills in network security together with the shortage of expertise in information security has been highlighted at an international level [4] and education and training has been proposed as a means of addressing the shortages of qualified personnel in industry [10].

Incorporation of industry-based training into academic courses is becoming more prevalent. There are many advantages supporting this adoption - for example, provision of skills which are immediately applicable in industry, attraction of more students to educational programs which provide marketable skills, and recognition of educational institutions as 'relevant' by organizations in industry.

The question arises – Is there extensive and justifiable support for the alignment of academic courses with professional accreditation and industry-based skills in information security or are we blindly embarking on this activity with little consideration of the consequences?

There is an ongoing debate of Universities claiming that they are providing education while industry courses only provide training. The students desire a University qualification but also want to have actual, practical and applicable skills that they can deploy immediately. They can thereby impress their employer with both education and training qualities. How best academia can accommodate vendor specific and professional accreditation training with academic learning outcomes and broader educational requirements, whilst still satisfying student desired outcomes and meeting international accreditation standards? This venue offers an opportunity to further discussion on these areas.

Some concerns and warnings (for a range of reasons) have also been presented on the topic. Academic institutions need to be aware of the risks associated with such moves and ensure they continue to offer information security education characterized by a balance of theory, knowledge and skills as part of the life-long learning process [4].

The lack of academic rigor and sound theoretical foundations are the concerns of numerous authors. Rannenberg [11] presents two main disadvantages of IT security product certification – the weaknesses of the underlying security models and the high cost of certification, and both these factors are also relevant to the discussion regarding professional certification of information security professionals. Valli [12] highlights the risks and warns against the consequences of the emphasis on accreditations and focus on industry certifications and encourages educational institutions to consider the consequences seriously - in particular the failing to provide sound foundations and become savants to vendors and industry bodies.

2. Proposed Workgroup Discussion

The first stage in the discussion will be to identify those industry certification, industry training, professional accreditation, and international standards, that have a direct relationship with information security education.

The second stage will be a discussion of the relevance of these in the meeting of academic objectives of tertiary education courses of information security. This will involve identifying the advantages and disadvantages, and weighing up the results.

The role of these professional accreditations and certifications in tertiary level academic qualifications will then be discussed, debating the extent to which these certifications should drive the design of academic programs.

The final stage will be developing guidelines and an action plan.

In order to encourage further discussion of the topic, it is intended that the results of the workshop will be written up into a paper for publication in the information security field.

References

1. Stanley, A.K., Information Security – challenges for the next millennium, in Yngstrom, L. & Carlsen, J., (Eds), *Information Security in Research and Business*, Chapman and Hall, London, (1997), pages 3-8
2. NSA, IACE Courseware Evaluation Programs, http://www.nsa.gov/ia/academia/iace.cfm
3. Rasmussen, C., Irvine, C., Dinolt, G., A Program for Education in Certification and Accreditation, in Irvine, C. & Armstrong, H. (Eds), *Security Education and Critical Infrastructures*, Kluwer Academic Publishers, (2003), pp 243
4. Armstrong, H. & Murray, I., Incorporating Vendor-based Training into Security Courses, *Proceedings of IEEE Systems, Man and Cybernetics Information Assurance Workshop*, June 2005
5. Clevenger, G. & Alexander, T., Practical Curriculum for the Future ISSO, *Proceedings of the 10th CISSE*, 2006, pages 8-13

6. Taylor, C., Alves-Foss, J. & Freeman, V., An Academic Perspective on the CNSS Standards: A Survey, *Proceedings of the 10th CISSE*, 2006, pages 39-46
7. Schembari, N.P., A University Course in Information Systems Risk Analysis/ Security Certification and Accreditation, *Proceedings of the 10th CISSE*, 2006, pages 22-30
8. Slay, J., Embedding Industry Standards within the Undergraduate IT Security Curriculum: An Australian Implementation, *Proceedings of the 8th CISSE,* 2004, pages 71-76
9. Conti, G., Hill, J., Lathrop, S., Alford, K. & Ragsdale, D., A Comprehensive Undergraduate Information Assurance Program, in C. Irvine and H. Armstrong (Eds), *Security Education and Critical Infrastructures*, Kluwer Academic Publishers, (2003), pp 243-260
10. Spalding, E., 2002, European ICT skills shortage still significant, despite economic woes, Comptia, available http://www.trainingpressreleases.com
11. Rannenberg, K., IT Security Certification and Criteria, in Qing, S. & Eloff, J., (Eds) *Information Security for Global Information Infrastructures*, Kluwer Academic Publishers (2000), pages 1-10
12. Valli, C., Industry Certifications, Challenges for the Conduct of University Security Based Courses, *Proceedings of the 4th Australian Information Warfare and Security Conference*, Adelaide, 2003

How to Design Computer Security Experiments

Sean Peisert[1] and Matt Bishop[2]

[1] Dept. of Computer Science & Engineering
University of California, San Diego
`peisert@cs.ucsd.edu`
[2] Department of Computer Science
University of California, Davis
`bishop@cs.ucdavis.edu`

Abstract. In this paper, we discuss the scientific method and how it can be applied to computer security experiments. We reiterate a number of general scientific principles, such as falsifiable hypotheses, scientific controls, reproducible results, and data quality.

1 Introduction

"Computer security is also a science. Its theory is based on mathematical constructions, analyses, and proofs. Its systems are built in accordance with the accepted practices of engineering. It uses inductive and deductive reasoning to examine the security of systems from key axioms and to discover underlying principles. These scientific principles can then be applied to untraditional situations and new theories, policies, and mechanisms." [1]

Recently, there has been considerable controversy about the rigor of some experimental work and of the validity of some data sets used in computer security research. In some cases, the problem stems from poor experimental technique. In other cases, it comes from trying to apply the results, which are valid over the selected data sets, to environments or situations not reflected by the data sets.

The experimental method is critical to placing computer science on a firm scientific and engineering basis. In this paper, we reiterate a number of the fundamental tenets of the scientific method and discuss how they apply to computer security.

The scientific method—testing a hypothesis by performing controlled experiments, resulting in measurable, empirical data—must be used to evaluate anything that cannot be proven by pure mathematics or logical syllogisms [AriCE].

---

[1] *Computer Security: Art and Science* [Bis03], p. xxxiii.

Please use the following format when citing this chapter:

Peisert, S., Bishop, M., 2007, in IFIP International Federation for Information Processing, Volume 237, Fifth World Conference on Information Security Education, eds. Futcher, L., Dodge, R., (Boston: Springer), pp. 141–148.

2   The Scientific Method

Classically "science" was performed through pure *deduction*. In the 17th century, the experimental method augmented the syllogism; thus, *induction* joined deduction. This method usually follows the following process [Kuh62,Wik07]:

1. Form hypothesis
2. Perform experiment and collect data.
3. Analyze data.
4. Interpret data and draw conclusions.
5. Depending on conclusions, return to #1 and iterate.

This process requires the procedures to have several qualities. The ones most relevant to computer security are:

1. *Falsifiable.* An experiment must be constructed to test a hypothesis [New87] that is both testable and falsifiable [Pop59].
2. *Controlled.* An experiment must have exactly one variable, or if an experiment has multiple variables, then it must be able to be separated into multiple experiments where exactly one variable at a time can be tested [Lin53].
3. *Reproducible.* An experiment must be reproducible, and results repeatable [Boy61].

One other quality that we do not focus on arises when experiments require that the results of using an automated process be checked. An example would be an experiment to determine whether an intrusion detection system can identify certain attacks. These experiments should be *blind*, so the experimenter does not know whether the data being given to the intrusion detection system contains the attacks. This eliminates any bias introduced unconsciously by the experimenter. When human subjects are used, it is equally important that the experiment be *double blind*, so that neither the experimenter nor the subjects know which subjects are the controls and which are not.

In addition to using the results of an experiment to test a hypothesis, one must validate that the experiment does indeed test the hypothesis. One interesting aspect of experiments in computer science is that, in order to obtain data from the experiment to analyze, one must typically *supply* data to the computer or process. The output data, which is to be analyzed to validate or refute the hypothesis, depends upon some attributes of the input data—the contents of that data, or some attributes such as the statistical distribution of inter-arrival times of messages. Thus, the truth or falsity of every hypothesis is to some extent conditioned on the input data set. That data must be selected appropriately. For example, if the hypothesis says something about the way a system works on the Internet, the data set must reflect the characteristics of Internet traffic. Hence, an additional step in testing a hypothesis is the validation of the input data set. This step is often overlooked, and general conclusions about the validity of a hypothesis are drawn from data drawn from a local environment.

We expand on these ideas briefly.

2.1 Falsifiable

If a hypothesis is falsifiable, it can produce a negative result. Two factors in a hypothesis being falsifiable are *observability* and *measurability*. If something cannot be observed (either directly or indirectly), it cannot be measured or studied. For example, the hypothesis that prayer increases the number of times that one's deity speaks to oneself is not falsifiable, because humans have thus far not developed methods of observing personal divine communication, and thus no experiment could prove the reported results wrong. What is observed must also be measurable. For example, the hypothesis that some software is secure is not measurable because "security" *per se* is not measurable. Saying that the software does not acquire the privileges of user X without requiring user X's password *is* measurable, because one can execute the software with different inputs, and see if the property holds.

A worm can be released and monitored on an isolated network to determine its rate of propagation in the face of specific controls. But simply observing the behavior of that worm in the "wild" will not determine this rate because other factors may confound the analysis. Such an experiment is not testing; it is observation. Similarly, observing that the stock market cycles are correlated with the number of active Internet worms does not mean that a causal relationship exists, because neither can be controlled to be tested. However, a hypothesis about such a relationship, followed by a controlled experiment *could* be valid.

2.2 Controlled

Consider the hypothesis, "if we use intrusion detection system X, we will catch 50% more attacks than with our competitor's product, Y." This leaves a number of open questions. What is an attack? Do both products look for the same type of attacks? Are the additional attacks captured at the expense of additional false positives? A tool that produces zero false positives *or* zero false negatives is trivial to design: either reject or accept every instance, respectively. Are both products tested against the same dataset? If the intrusion detection systems are set up on a public access network, are they reading data from the same locations on the network? Are the IP addresses of their hosts similar? Are the operating systems and versions of their hosts identical? Answering "no" to any of these questions means that the experiment has more than one uncontrolled variable, and therefore, conclusions drawn about the effect of changing one variable are suspect. These questions cannot be enumerated without knowing the nature of the hypothesis and environment in which the experiments will take place, because experimental setup varies widely according to the aims of the research. But the questions must nevertheless be asked by the researcher when designing their experiments.

2.3 Reproducible

Consider the problem of obtaining data sets for analyzing the ability of intrusion detection systems to detect attacks accurately. One of the most common methods is to implement a *honeypot*, or a network of honeypots—known as a *honeynet* [Spi03] —and to wait to be attacked. Unfortunately, for this type of data set to be meaningful, one must show that attacks launched against honeypots are representative of attacks launched against production systems and networks.

Data sets are frequently not published, so the validity of the dataset itself cannot be verified. Among the reasons for this are that the data is proprietary, or contains sensitive information such as login names and passwords, or patient names and medical conditions, or bank account numbers and records of financial transactions. In some cases, data must be kept confidential by law. Even if this data were sanitized, one must show that the sanitization did not alter properties that affect the analysis.

These constraints lead to the development of artificial data sets that match the relevant statistics of real data sets. But what are the "relevant" statistics? An artificial data set may match first-order statistics, but not second-order statistics, of real data. So an experiment about a system that relies only on first-order statistics can use this artificial data set to produce meaningful results. The same cannot be said for a system that uses second-order statistics.

To summarize, enabling others to reproduce experiments requires that:

1. the conditions (assumptions, controls, and variables) of the experiment must be documented thoroughly enough so that the dataset can be re-created, to determine its validity, and
2. the data used must be saved, so that both the tools and methods in question, as well as new tools, can be tested against the existing data.

3 An Example Experiment in Computer Security

As an example, suppose we are testing a new firewall. The vendor claims that it is secure, and can protect any system behind it. However, this is not a question, but a statement. To clarify the claim, the vendor suggests the following hypothesis:

Hypothesis 1: Only an extraordinarily skilled attacker can break into our firewall.

Unfortunately, this hypothesis is not falsifiable, because if an attacker does breach the firewall, the vendor can claim the attacker is "extraordinarily skilled." So, to be falsifiable, we either need to quantify "extraordinarily skilled" or use some other metric.

Accordingly, we refine the question by returning to the original claim and consider what "secure" and "protect any system behind it" mean. After some discussion with the vendor, it becomes clear that the vendor is assuming that access to the controls of the firewall is from a physically connected terminal, so the only avenues of attack are through the traffic transiting the firewall.

Hypothesis 2: The firewall accepts all well-formed packets and sessions, and handles malformed packets and sessions as documented in the firewall's manual.

This hypothesis is both testable and falsifiable. We can bombard the firewall with packets, and begin a session and send incorrect packets as part of the session. If the firewall handles them properly (by discarding them, logging them, and possibly resetting the connection), then the hypothesis is true. If the firewall handles them improperly (by crashing, or by allowing them to corrupt its network stack), then the hypothesis is false.

We now consider an experiment to test the hypothesis. There are two variables involved in any such experiment: the firewall configuration, which dictates what packets should be allowed to transit the firewall, and the data set of incoming packets. We must therefore eliminate one variable.

If the goal of the experiment is to determine whether a particular configuration is the most effective for preventing some class of packets from transiting the firewall, then the variable is the firewall configuration. If the goal of the experiment is to determine whether the firewall correctly handles malformed packets and sessions, the variable is the data set of packets sent to the firewall. As we are interested in the former, we use the default firewall configuration supplied by the vendor and vary the data sent to the firewall.

Experiment 1: Connect the firewall to a local network and send packets, some malformed and some parts of malformed sessions, through the firewall. Record the packets and the firewall's responses.

This experiment is, unfortunately, not reproducible. Although the packets have been recorded, ancillary characteristics (such as timing) have not been. If the packets are arriving faster than the firewall can process them, the firewall may drop those packets or allow them to overwrite packets in the processing buffer, causing valid packets to appear malformed. So we must refine the experiment further:

Experiment 2: Connect the firewall to a local network and send packets, some malformed and some parts of malformed sessions, though the firewall. Record the network traffic, including timings, and the firewall's responses.

This experiment is reproducible, because anyone can take the network traces and reproduce the traffic. Unfortunately, its utility is questionable. To see why, we must consider the type of data set involved.

This particular data set is generated synthetically. But the firewall will not be used on synthetic data; it will be connected to real networks, with real traffic. How do we know that the data set accurately captures the relevant characteristics of the data that the firewall must handle in practice?

The relevance of the question lies in the nature of the firewall. If it is stateless, then each individual packet is handled independently of any other packet. The distribution of timings within the network traffic, though, may vary from site to site. A site whose main network activity is email will have a different distribution of inter-packet arrivals and departures than will a site that uses voice over IP, or transmits or receives videos on demand. The variance may impact the ability of the firewall to handle packets.

However, as the firewall is claimed to be able to detect malformed sessions, it is probably a stateful firewall; if not, how could it detect that packets, well-formed in and of themselves, were in a sequence that violated the state transitions of a well-formed session? This raises other questions, such as whether the distribution of packet content, length, and other attributes could affect the way the firewall handles packets. In this case, the data set needs to capture the statistics of *all* relevant attributes of the data. This strongly suggests using real data, not synthetic data.

Like the question of timings, the distribution of different types and sizes of packets and sessions varies among institutions. Hence our experiment cannot confirm the hypothesis in general; it can only confirm (or refute) it for the particular data set used. It is our responsibility to characterize that data set sufficiently to allow others to determine whether our answer is meaningful to them. As an example, if we used traffic from a site that only sent email over the Internet, and had no other network traffic, our results would not be particularly useful to a site where the network traffic were substantially different.

This, incidentally, is an often-overlooked point. One should not characterize network traffic in terms of the nature of the site from which it was obtained. Universities, for example, do not generate the same type of traffic. A college that focuses on teaching, and does not have a computer science major, might have predominantly web and email traffic. A college that has a computer science department actively researching new network protocols, and working with several commercial firms and the government, will generate a large amount of network traffic that is not easily characterized. So saying some network traces come from an academic site does not characterize it adequately enough to know *what* characteristics it has.

The best way to characterize our data set is to release it. In addition to enabling others to do exactly what we did, others can obtain their own data, determine if its characteristics match ours, and if so, then use it to reproduce the experiment. It also points out limits on our results: if the characteristics do not match, our results may or may not be valid. But providing results that can be shown to be invalid is good science: it allows claims to be refuted or refined, and thus progress made. Providing results that *can* be invalidated is ultimately necessary to develop results that ultimately withstand the test of time.

4   Conclusions

> DR. JONES: *"Archaeology is the search for fact. Not truth. If it's truth you're looking for, Dr. Tyree's philosophy class is right down the hall."*
> —*Indiana Jones and the Last Crusade* (1989)

The results of experiments can be misleading, especially when statistical analysis is involved. Darrell Huff's marvelous example about increases in California teachers' salaries causing increases in the profits of Nevada casinos underscores the difference between correlation and causation [Huf54]. Simply observing the effects of an experiment without first positing a hypothesis can give absurd results, such as an observation that "stock market cycles and sunspot cycles are roughly in sync, and the stock market peaks and dips slightly before sunspot cycles," so therefore, "stock market cycles cause sunspots." On the other hand, if a researcher could run an experiment in which she had control over either the sunspots or the stock market, then she could form the hypothesis that "stock market cycles cause sunspots" and conduct valid experiments to confirm or refute that hypothesis.

As an example from computer security, a worm can be released and monitored on an isolated network to determine its rate of propagation in the face of specific controls. But simply observing the behavior of that worm in the "wild" will not determine this rate because other factors may confound the analysis. Such an experiment is not testing; it is observation. Similarly, observing that the stock market cycles are correlated with the number of active Internet worms does not mean that a causal relationship exists, because neither can be controlled to be tested. However, a hypothesis about such a relationship, followed by a controlled experiment *could* be valid.

Sometimes there is insufficient data to form a useful or interesting hypothesis. In this case, experimentation can guide the researcher toward developing a hypothesis to test. This type of experiment is fundamentally different than the type discussed before, because it does not "prove" anything. As long as the nature of the experiment is clear, and the results are understood to be useful only in forming hypotheses that *other* experiments will test, this type of exploratory experimentation contributes to the advancement of the field. When the results of these exploratory experiments are used to validate hypotheses derived from their results, though, one reasons circularly—"we obtained the following results, which led us to hypothesize X, and we can confirm X because of the results of the experiment"—and so there is in reality no proof. An independent experiment is required to test the hypothesis.

In order to claim scientifically valid and justifiable results, computer security experiments must follow the scientific method, using high-quality, repeatable and verifiable methods and data sets. Only in this way, non-scientists in the "real world," such as those who make decisions about the security of electronic voting machines, hospital operating room equipment, and airplane software can trust the research and researchers whose technology they are using.

References

[AriCE] Aristotle. *Organon*. 100 B.C.E.

[Bis03] Matt Bishop. *Computer Security: Art and Science*. Addison-Wesley Professional, Boston, MA, 2003.

[Boy61] Robert Boyle. The Unsuccessful Experiment. In *Certain Physiological Essays*. Henry Herringman, London, 1661.

[Huf54] Darrell Huff. *How to Lie With Statistics*. Norton, 1954.

[Kuh62] Thomas S. Kuhn. *The Structure of Scientific Revolutions*. University of Chicago Press, Chicago, 1962.

[Lin53] James Lind. *A Treatise of the Scurvy*. Sands, Murray, and Cochran for A Kincaid and A Donaldson, 1753.

[New87] Sir Isaac Newton. *Philosophiae Naturalis Principia Mathematica*. The Royal Society, 1687.

[Pop59] Karl Raimund Popper. *The Logic of Scientific Discovery*. Routledge, 1959.

[Spi03] Lance Spitzner. The Honeynet Project: Trapping the Hackers. *IEEE Security & Privacy*, 1(2):15–23, Mar–Apr 2003.

[Wik07] The Free Encyclopedia Wikipedia. Scientific method. http://en.wikipedia.org/w/index.php?title=Scientific_method&oldid=104300855, January 30 09:59 UTC 2007.